North American Indian Wars

Other Books in the Turning Points Series:

Turning|Points
IN WORLD HISTORY

North American Indian Wars

Don Nardo, *Book Editor*

David L. Bender, *Publisher*
Bruno Leone, *Executive Editor*
Bonnie Szumski, *Editorial Director*

Greenhaven Press, Inc., San Diego, California

Library of Congress Cataloging-in-Publication Data

North American Indian wars / Don Nardo, book editor.
    p.   cm. — (Turning points in world history)
  Includes bibliographical references and index.
  ISBN 1-56510-959-7 (lib. : alk. paper). —
ISBN 1-56510-958-9 (pbk. : alk. paper)
  1. Indians of North America—Wars. 2. Indians of North America—Government relations. 3. Indians, Treatment of—United States—History. I. Nardo, Don, 1947–   . II. Series: Turning points in world history (Greenhaven Press)
E81.N69 1999
973—dc21   98-47353
                                                                    CIP

Cover photo: © Superstock

©1999 by Greenhaven Press, Inc.
P.O. Box 289009, San Diego, CA 92198-9009

Printed in the U.S.A.

Contents

mile-long trek for freedom, one of history's most daring and effective fighting retreats.

Chapter 3: The Disastrous Impact of White Conquest

span of only one or two generations, white hunters brought the buffalo to the brink of extinction, robbing thousands of Indians of their traditional livelihoods.

Chapter 4: Epilogue: Legacy of the Indian Wars

Foreword

Certain past events stand out as pivotal, as having effects and outcomes that change the course of history. These events are often referred to as turning points. Historian Louis L. Snyder provides this useful definition:

> A turning point in history is an event, happening, or stage which thrusts the course of historical development into a different direction. By definition a turning point is a great event, but it is even more—a great event with the explosive impact of altering the trend of man's life on the planet.

History's turning points have taken many forms. Some were single, brief, and shattering events with immediate and obvious impact. The invasion of Britain by William the Conqueror in 1066, for example, swiftly transformed that land's political and social institutions and paved the way for the rise of the modern English nation. By contrast, other single events were deemed of minor significance when they occurred, only later recognized as turning points. The assassination of a little-known European nobleman, Archduke Franz Ferdinand, on June 28, 1914, in the Bosnian town of Sarajevo was such an event; only after it touched off a chain reaction of political-military crises that escalated into the global conflict known as World War I did the murder's true significance become evident.

Other crucial turning points occurred not in terms of a few hours, days, months, or even years, but instead as evolutionary developments spanning decades or even centuries. One of the most pivotal turning points in human history, for instance—the development of agriculture, which replaced nomadic hunter-gatherer societies with more permanent settlements—occurred over the course of many generations. Still other great turning points were neither events nor developments, but rather revolutionary new inventions and innovations that significantly altered social customs and ideas, military tactics, home life, the spread of knowledge, and the human condition in general. The developments of writing, gunpowder, the printing press, antibiotics, the electric light, atomic energy, television, and the computer, the last two of which have recently ushered in the world-altering information age, represent only some of these innovative turning points.

Each anthology in the Greenhaven Turning Points in World History series presents a group of essays chosen for their accessibility. The anthology's structure also enhances this accessibility. First, an introductory essay provides a general overview of the principal events and figures involved, placing the topic in its historical context. The essays that follow explore various aspects in more detail, some targeting political trends and consequences, others social, literary, cultural, and/or technological ramifications, and still others pivotal leaders and other influential figures. To aid the reader in choosing the material of immediate interest or need, each essay is introduced by a concise summary of the contributing writer's main themes and insights.

In addition, each volume contains extensive research tools, including a collection of excerpts from primary source documents pertaining to the historical events and figures under discussion. In the anthology on the French Revolution, for example, readers can examine the works of Rousseau, Voltaire, and other writers and thinkers whose championing of human rights helped fuel the French people's growing desire for liberty; the French *Declaration of the Rights of Man and Citizen*, presented to King Louis XVI by the French National Assembly on October 2, 1789; and eyewitness accounts of the attack on the royal palace and the horrors of the Reign of Terror. To guide students interested in pursuing further research on the subject, each volume features an extensive bibliography, which for easy access has been divided into separate sections by topic. Finally, a comprehensive index allows readers to scan and locate content efficiently. Each of the anthologies in the Greenhaven Turning Points in World History series provides students with a complete, detailed, and enlightening examination of a crucial historical watershed.

Introduction: The United States Versus the Indians

When the United States declared its independence in 1776, it consisted of a string of former British colonies stretching north to south along the eastern North American coast. At the time, American leaders realized that westward expansion was inevitable. But they assumed that it would be a slow, methodical process taking many generations, perhaps even several centuries. They could not then remotely envision how huge and rapid the westward march of white settlers would actually become, nor could they predict that it would shatter in a matter of decades the entire Native American civilization that had existed for millennia. Hundreds of Indian tribes, the continent's original inhabitants, stood in the way of what became a veritable steamroller of American expansion. This made them, in the eyes of most whites who saw themselves as superior to Indians, an obstacle to be removed at whatever cost was necessary.

For Native Americans, that cost turned out to be enormous and devastating. Before white Europeans began colonizing North America, the area now encompassed by the continental United States was inhabited by at least 1 million Indians, organized into some six hundred separate, flourishing tribes. By the time the Indian wars ended in the 1890s, dozens of tribes had been totally or nearly annihilated. The rest had been decimated and demoralized, and the overall Native American population had been reduced to less than 400,000. "The impact of white conquest on this culture was . . . disastrous," state scholars John Tebbel and Keith Jennison.

> Their lands gone, they were confined for the most part to reservations in [the] western United States, victims of discriminatory laws enacted by white bigots and of governmental neglect and mismanagement of their affairs. . . . The conquest itself may be explained by the inexorable [relentless] march of history, but the manner of its accomplishment cannot be

excused. From the first atrocities of the Spanish, French, and English explorers and colonizers to the final, frightful massacre of Indian women and children at Wounded Knee in 1890, the white man's war against the red man is a record to match in savagery, if not in scope, anything the refinements of twentieth-century civilized warfare have produced.[1]

Why was the white victory so complete and final? Simply put, the whites were more numerous and unified and also possessed more advanced industry and technology than the Indians. So the tribes had no real chance of winning the series of wars and battles they fought with the United States from the late eighteenth to late nineteenth centuries. Their defeat in these conflicts ensured that the United States would ultimately stretch from the Atlantic to the Pacific. Because they helped make possible the emergence of a U.S. nation of continental proportions, an entity that went on to become the mightiest and most influential country on earth, the American Indian wars marked a crucial turning point in world history.

Whites "Naturally Superior" to Indians?

It must be noted that eighteenth- and nineteenth-century white Americans did not initiate the systematic and relentless decimation of Native American cultures. This process of pushing the Indians farther and farther westward and confiscating their lands had been set in motion by the English, French, and other Europeans who had begun colonizing North America's eastern seaboard in the early 1600s. At first, contacts between Native Americans and the settlers of Jamestown, Plymouth, and other early white beachheads were largely peaceful. For instance, the Indians welcomed and helped the English immigrants who established the Jamestown colony on the shore of Chesapeake Bay in Virginia in 1607. The colony started with 900 people, but the first winters were harsh and starvation and disease killed some 750 colonists. The local Indians, members of the Algonquin confederacy of two hundred villages and thirty-two tribes, observed the whites' plight and, out of pity and concern, gave them food and other supplies. For a few short years, the Algonquin and colonists lived together in peace.

However, as white populations grew and required more land to sustain themselves, the peace was shattered. Much of the violence stemmed from the colonists' cultural arrogance and religious intolerance. First, they believed that they had the right to dominate the Indians and to take their lands because whites were "naturally superior" to nonwhites. In the eyes of most whites, Indians were wild, uncivilized savages who could not be trusted. "They have the shapes of men and may be of the human species," wrote a white resident of eighteenth-century Pennsylvania,

> but certainly in their present state they approach nearer the character of Devils; take an Indian, is there any faith in him? Can you bind him by favors? Can you trust his word or confide in his promise? When he makes war upon you, when he takes you prisoner . . . will he spare you? [The author concludes that the answer is no.] In this he departs from the law of nature. . . . On this principle are not the whole Indian nations murderers?[2]

Religious beliefs also played an important role in anti-Indian prejudice. The whites were Christians, with strong devotion to the Bible and the existence of one all-powerful, and decidedly Christian, god. Convinced that theirs was the only true faith, they looked down on Indian religious notions of nature gods and spirits as primitive and childish. It seemed, therefore, not only morally justified for whites to control both Indians and Indian lands but also a divinely inspired duty to convert the "red heathens" to Christianity. Typical was this patronizing speech made by a Boston missionary to a chief of the Seneca, a tribe indigenous to northern New York:

> I have come . . . to instruct you how to worship the Great Spirit agreeably to his mind and will, and to preach to you the gospel of his son, Jesus Christ. There is but one religion, and but one way to serve God, and if you do not embrace the right way, you cannot be happy hereafter. You have never worshipped the Great Spirit in a manner acceptable to him;

but have, all your lives, been in great errors and darkness. To endeavor to remove these errors, and open your eyes, so that you might see clearly, is my business with you.[3]

Images of Native Americans as uncivilized, savage, untrustworthy, and ungodly constituted only part of a growing collection of stereotypes perpetrated and widely accepted by whites. White settlers were seen as inherently peaceful and benevolent, a race of valiant, hardworking, and God-fearing people attempting to tame a hostile wilderness. In contrast, Indians were pictured as warlike and bloodthirsty by nature; any Indian resistance to white expansion was therefore viewed as hostile, unjustified, treacherous, and murderous.

Land Ownership and Jefferson's Vision

These stereotypes helped to justify white expansion and fueled the engines of the growing concept of "manifest destiny," the idea that white Americans were destined to control all the lands lying between the Atlantic and Pacific Oceans. However, the main white justification for taking former Indian lands was the marked difference in the ways the two races used these lands. The whites felt that Native Americans could not lay claim to land that they merely "roamed over" and "hunted on." By contrast, according to this view, white settlers "developed" the land by farming it, building cities on it, and bringing to it the fruits of "progress" and "civilization." (These views conveniently ignored the facts that many Native American tribes farmed the land, built permanent villages on it, and recognized established tribal boundaries.) President Theodore Roosevelt (served 1901–1909), who in regard to Indians was essentially an apologist for white appropriation of their lands, later summed up the white view this way:

It cannot be too often insisted that they [the Indians] did not own the land; or, at least, that their ownership was merely such as that claimed often by our own white hunters. . . . To recognize the Indian ownership of the limitless prairies and forests of this continent—that is, to consider the dozen squalid savages who hunted at long intervals over a territory of a thousand square miles as owning it outright—necessarily implies a similar recognition of the claims of every white hunter, squatter, horse-thief, or wandering cattle-man. . . . The different tribes have always been utterly unable to define their own boundaries. . . . The tribes were warlike and bloodthirsty, jealous of each other and of the whites; they claimed the land for their hunting grounds, but their claims all conflicted with one another; their knowledge of their own boundaries was so indefinite that they were always willing, for inadequate compensation, to sell land to which they had merely the vaguest title [of ownership]; and yet, when once they had received the goods, were generally reluctant to make over [develop] what they could.[4]

Indeed, differing concepts of and disputes over land ownership and use rested at the heart of the struggles between white and Native Americans. A core cause of conflicts between the two peoples ever since the onset of European settlement of North America, this dispute greatly intensified in the late 1700s, when the infant United States began fulfilling its manifest destiny and pushing westward. The future of the continent now depended on the answers to two basic questions. First, could whites and Indians find a way to coexist in the American frontier? Second, assuming that they could not coexist, could the Indians stop the inevitable and relentless white advance?

Initial attempts by both sides to answer these questions are conveniently summarized in the visions of Thomas Jefferson, the third U.S. president (born in 1743 in the English colony of Virginia), and Tecumseh, a Shawnee chief (born about 1768 near the current site of Springfield, Ohio). Jefferson viewed the western march of white settlers as necessary for the growth and prosperity of the United States. He believed that the country's future would be shaped by independent, hardworking farmers, God's "chosen people," who would set an example for other Americans.

Jefferson was well aware that westward settlement would cause land disputes with Native Americans. But he fully accepted the argument that tribal failure to develop the land, using the white definition of such development, negated any

Indian claims of ownership. He saw two basic possibilities for the Indians' future. They could either learn to become independent farmers in the white sense and slowly assimilate into white culture, or they could find new lands to live in. Jefferson assumed that because many Indians hunted, fished, and otherwise lived off the land, they could live anywhere, so why not let them move farther west, beyond the Mississippi, to make room for white settlers? In 1803, he wrote to the governor of the Ohio Territory:

> They [the Indians] will in time either incorporate with us as citizens of the United States or remove beyond the Mississippi. The former is certainly the termination of their history most happy for themselves, but, in the whole course of this, it is essential to cultivate their love. As to their fear, we presume that our strength and their weakness is now so visible that they must see that we have only to shut our hand to crush them, and that all our liberalities to them proceed from motives of pure humanity only.[5]

This statement shows that Jefferson, like most other whites of his time, had already concluded that the Indians were a doomed race, or at least the Indian way of life east of the Mississippi was doomed; the red race, Jefferson sincerely believed, could still save itself by retreating westward. He did not take into account, or perhaps did not care, that the Indians who lived west of the great river might resent eastern Indians entering their territories. At least, in his view, whites and Indians could thereafter stay out of each other's way and coexist on the same continent in peace. In fact, he more than once expressed the naïve, wholly unrealistic idea that the west was large and bountiful enough to accommodate all, white and red alike, for hundreds of generations to come.

The Lost Cause of Indian Unity

Jefferson's vision, a strange mixture of well-meaning paternal concern for his "red children" and coldly cruel acceptance of dispossessing them of their lands and way of life, was, in the words of noted historian Stephen Ambrose, "all a pipe dream." One may "as well try to stop an avalanche as to stop the moving frontier."[6] Like a number of other Indian leaders, Tecumseh, after trying to negotiate with and fighting whites for many years, grasped the reality that white westward expansion would continue relentlessly and indefinitely. And unlike Jefferson, he realized that there was not enough frontier land to accommodate both Indians and whites. One race or the other would have to give way, and there was every reason to believe that the western Indians would suffer the same fate the eastern ones had in colonial days. "Where today are the Pequot?" Tecumseh asked other Indians.

> Where are the Narragansett, the Mohican, the Pocanet, and other powerful [eastern] tribes of our people? They have vanished before the avarice [greed] and oppression of the white man, as snow before the summer sun. . . . Will we let ourselves be destroyed in our turn, without making an effort worthy of our race? Shall we, without a struggle, give up our homes, our lands, bequeathed to us by the Great Spirit? The graves of our dead and everything that is dear and sacred to us? . . . I know you will say with me, Never! Never![7]

In Tecumseh's view, the only way to stop the white tidal wave was for all Indians to unite. And he dreamed of forging one mighty alliance of all the tribes from Canada to the Gulf of Mexico. When some Indians gave in and sold their lands to the whites, Tecumseh bitterly responded:

> The only way to stop this evil is for the red men to unite in claiming a common and equal right in the land, as it was at first, and should be now—for it was never divided, but belongs to all. No tribe has the right to sell, even to each other, much less to strangers. . . . *Sell a country! Why not sell the air, the great sea, as well as the earth?* Did not the Great Spirit make them all for the use of his children?[8]

At first, Tecumseh was moderately successful in his efforts to unite the tribes. In 1790, he and his Shawnee joined forces with Miami, Potawatomi, and Chippewa under the Miami chief Little Turtle and decisively defeated an army of 1,400 U.S. troops in the Ohio Valley. This Native American alliance followed up with an even more impressive victory about a year later along Ohio's Wabash River. The fierce three-hour battle ended in the most one-sided Indian victory up to that time; the white soldiers counted some 630 killed and 300 wounded, while Indian casualties numbered fewer than 100.

These victories marked the high point of Tecumseh's anti-white campaign, however. New and larger U.S. armies kept marching against him, and despite his tireless and courageous efforts, he was simply unable to convince enough tribes and warriors to join his pan-Indian crusade. In 1794, General Anthony Wayne delivered Tecumseh's forces a devastating defeat at Fallen Timbers, near the western shore of Lake Erie. This event marked an important turning point in the history of the Indian wars. In its wake, thousands of whites began pouring into Ohio and Indiana, and most of the local chiefs, perceiving that they had no choice, signed a treaty granting most of the region to the United States.

To his credit, Tecumseh refused to sign the treaty and continued his efforts to halt the white advance. But it became increasingly clear that his cause was hopeless. In October 1813, during the War of 1812 between the United States and Britain, in which Tecumseh allied himself with the latter against the former, the great chief was killed in battle. His dream of a mighty Indian alliance against the whites died with him. After his passing, the northeastern tribes proved too disunited to resist the white advance. In a pattern that would be repeated again and again across the continent in the coming years, some tribes made peace with the Americans and helped them fight other tribes, while those tribes that continued to resist white expansion were defeated and uprooted one by one.

Removal and Relocation

Ultimately, as Jefferson had foreseen, all tribes that were not "crushed," as he had put it, were pushed beyond the Mississippi. Beginning in the 1820s, the U.S. government delegated a special region for Indian relocation, which became known, appropriately, as Indian Country (or Indian Territory). At its greatest extent it included the lands now en-

2786810

compassed by the states of Oklahoma, Kansas, and Nebraska. According to the U.S. government's new policy, any tribes that stood in the way of white expansion would have to be removed, by force if necessary, and preferably relocated to Indian Country.

The leading U.S. figure in implementing the policy of Indian removal in these years was Andrew Jackson, a noted military officer and later president (1829–1837). His goal was to create separate living spheres for whites and Indians, motivated in large part by his belief that Indians were inferior and barbaric. Like Jefferson, Jackson failed to see that by pushing Indians off their land, he was depriving them of their livelihood. He too thought that they could simply move anywhere and find some way to live off the land. But to the Indians, removal caused untold misery and the destruction of entire ways of life. Thousands of people were forced to abandon their ancestral homes and move to distant, unfamiliar territories.

The first Indians Jackson dealt with were the Creek, who inhabited what are now Georgia and Alabama. The Creek Wars of 1813–1814 ended in the total defeat of the tribe and the confiscation of over 23 million acres of former Creek lands by the United States. At first, the surviving Creek were forced onto small reservations in Alabama, but later, after Jackson became president, the government forced most of them to move to Indian Country. In 1829, a Creek chief, Speckled Snake, bitterly complained:

He [the white man] became our Great Father. He loved his red children, but he said: "You must move a little farther, lest by accident I tread on you.". . . Now he says, "The land you live on is not yours. Go beyond the Mississippi; there is game; there you may remain while the grass grows and the rivers run.". . . Brothers, I have listened to a great many talks from our Great Father. But they always began and ended in this—"Get a little farther; you are too near me."[9]

Jackson also fought, defeated, and later relocated other southeastern tribes. Among them were the Seminole of northern Florida, who fiercely and valiantly resisted U.S.

troops for more than two decades before being overrun. Between 1835 and 1842, the U.S. government shipped about three thousand Seminole to Indian Country, although another two thousand members of the tribe escaped into the Florida swamps, where whites could root them out only with great difficulty. Removal of other tribes, including the Cherokee, Choctaw, and Chickasaw, proceeded much more efficiently, however. Efficiently, that is, from the white point of view, for relocation caused these Indians to endure terrible hardships. For example, when six thousand Cherokee moved in 1817 from South Carolina to the Arkansas Territory, then part of Indian Country, the Osage, who inhabited that region, saw the newcomers as intruders. The Cherokee and Osage went to war in 1821 and both sides suffered heavy casualties.

Perhaps the most infamous case of Indian removal was that involving the Cherokee in Georgia. They refused to move, even after their South Carolinian brethren had done so. This prompted Jackson's successor in the White House, Martin Van Buren, to take drastic action. In May 1838 he ordered seven thousand U.S. troops and Georgia state militia to remove the Cherokee by whatever means necessary. Soldiers quietly surrounded Cherokee homes, then surprised and dragged away the occupants, after which crowds of whites looted and burned the empty houses. Within a week, the troops rounded up over seventeen thousand Cherokee and began transporting them west. In this forced march, which came to be known as the "Trail of Tears," dozens of Indians died of starvation, exposure, or illness each day. A white witness later recalled:

> Many of the aged Indians were suffering extremely from the fatigue of the journey. . . . Several were then quite ill. . . . The sick and the feeble were carried in wagons. . . . Even aged females, apparently nearly ready to drop into the grave, were traveling with heavy burdens attached to the back—on the sometimes frozen ground, and sometimes muddy streets, with no covering for the feet except what nature had given them. . . . They buried fourteen or fifteen [Cherokee] at every stopping place.[10]

In all, more than four thousand Cherokee died before the tribe reached its destination in Indian Country in 1839.

From the Long Walk to the Little Bighorn

The Indian wars in other parts of the continental United States followed patterns similar to those of the northeast and southeast. The lure of land to farm and develop brought a steady stream of white settlers into the western plains and the northwest. And other lures—gold and other mineral wealth and natural resources—induced many whites to move into Indian lands in the Dakotas, the southwestern desert regions, and California. In most of these regions, the Indians at first resisted, at times heroically, but in the end they were overwhelmed. In the 1850s, the U.S. army clashed with the Yakima, Walla Walla, and Cayuse tribes in the Oregon Territory (now Oregon and Washington); the Apache and Ute in the New Mexico Territory (now New Mexico and Arizona); and the Lakota Sioux, Cheyenne, and Comanche on the Great Plains. In the early 1860s, war continued with the Apache and engulfed another large southwestern tribe—the Navajo. After the Navajo were defeated in 1864, the army forced some thirty-five hundred members of the tribe to march (in what came to be called the "Long Walk") to a relocation camp in eastern New Mexico.[11]

While many other tribes, like the Navajo, suffered defeat, relocation, and/or confinement on reservations, some Indians were simply slaughtered in cold blood. Cherokee/Creek scholar Tom Holm, of the University of Arizona, describes two of the most outrageous examples:

On November 29, 1864, Colonel John M. Chivington led his Third Colorado Cavalry Regiment in an attack on a Cheyenne and Arapaho camp at Sand Creek, a tributary of the Arkansas River in southeastern Colorado. Black Kettle, the Cheyenne leader, had just concluded negotiations on a new peace treaty when Chivington's men attacked. Two hundred Cheyennes died in the onslaught, but, what was worse, Chivington's men dismembered Cheyenne corpses and brought hundreds of body parts back to Denver to be put on display at the local theater. Attacks on tribes by civilian irregulars, however, were even more horrible than those made by regular army troops. In 1871 at Camp Grant, Arizona, for example, a Tucson citizens' group killed and scalped most of the Apache males in the camp, and then raped, murdered, and scalped the women. They took the children to be sold into slavery.[12]

These massacres and others like them, along with continued white encroachment into Indian lands, inspired the remaining Plains tribes to step up their resistance against the whites. War parties of Sioux, Cheyenne, Arapaho, and other tribes regularly raided white outposts and wagon trains. In response, the U.S. army mounted one campaign after another against them. In the late 1860s and into the 1870s, numerous skirmishes, battles, and massacres took place on the plains as Kiowa, Comanche, Sioux, and others desperately struggled to protect their hunting grounds and way of life.

The most celebrated battle of the period, and probably the most famous of all battles between Indians and whites, was the defeat of George Armstrong Custer and the Seventh Cavalry near the Little Bighorn River (in southern Montana) in 1876. Custer was trying to destroy a huge encampment of allied Plains tribes. After dividing his forces in an attempt to attack the camp from several angles, his own contingent was surrounded and wiped out by warriors led by Crazy Horse and other chiefs.

The story of the battle has been retold, reconstructed, and depicted almost endlessly ever since in books and movies. But the actual details of the event are still disputed, partly because none of Custer's 267 men survived to tell the tale. A recently discovered narrative by a soldier serving in an army unit that fought on another side of the Indian camp is fascinating and valuable for its insights into Custer's overall campaign, but the author did not actually witness the Seventh Cavalry's demise.[13] Several accounts purportedly by Indians who fought in or observed the battle survived orally and were later written down in English; although some of these accounts are vague or contradictory, a number of others support reconstructions by military historians and are likely accurate. According to a Cheyenne chief, Brave Wolf, "It was hard fighting; very hard all the time. I have been in many hard fights, but never saw such brave men."[14] Crow King, a Sioux, concurred in his own account, which maintains that when Custer's men found themselves surrounded they dismounted and fought on foot:

> They tried to hold onto their horses, but as we pressed closer they let go their horses. We crowded them toward our main camp and killed them all. They kept in order and fought like brave warriors as long as they had a man left.[15]

Defeat and Subjugation

The exact details of this great Native American victory aside, the fact is that its strategic importance was nullified by subsequent events. For reasons unknown, the tribes involved did not, as they should have, remain united and follow up with coordinated attacks on other army units in the region. Instead, they disbanded and went their separate ways, virtually ensuring that the whites could continue their own routine strategy of picking them off one by one. Also, white society indignantly and angrily viewed the battle as a "massacre" by "bloodthirsty savages"; this led the U.S. government to step up its campaigns of revenge and conquest against the Sioux and other western tribes.

In the following decade or so, therefore, in what proved to be the last phase of the American Indian wars, one tribe after another was surrounded, defeated, and subjugated. Survivors were usually herded onto reservations. Yet even after such forced relocation, some tribes courageously continued to resist. About a year after Custer's defeat, the Nez Percé, under Chief Joseph, escaped from their Idaho reservation and made a daring attempt to reach Canada and freedom. After several times outwitting or fighting off the army units sent to capture them, they came within only thirty miles of achieving their goal; in the end, however, they had no choice but surrender.

At the very same time that the Nez Percé made their bid for freedom, three hundred Cheyenne, led by Chief Dull Knife, escaped from their own reservation and tried to return to their ancestral lands in Montana. With some ten thousand soldiers and three thousand white civilians chasing them, the small band traveled over fifteen hundred miles before being cornered and captured.

Groups of Apache warriors in the deserts of New Mexico and Arizona also refused to be confined on reservations. Under their war leader Geronimo, the Chiricahua Apache waged effective guerrilla warfare against the U.S. Army throughout the late 1870s and early 1880s. Geronimo managed to hold out until 1886, when an army of five thousand, led by General George Crook, forced him to surrender, an event that finally made it safe for massive white settlement of the Southwest.

The final major battle of the Indian wars took place four years later. Sensing that their civilization was nearing extinction, many Indians resorted in desperation to an unusual new religious belief that promised the salvation of their race. Called the Ghost Dance, it became popular on most of the Plains reservations in 1890. It predicted that, through magical powers, many whites would die and the Indians would push the rest eastward into the ocean. What is more, the leaders of the Ghost Dance claimed, wearing special shirts during the faith's ceremonies would make Indians immune to white soldiers' bullets. In a speech to his followers, one of these leaders, Short Bull, a Sioux, declared:

> If the soldiers surround you four deep, three of you, on whom I have put holy shirts, will sing a song, which I have taught you, around them, when some of them will drop dead. Then the rest will start to run, but their horses will sink into the earth. The riders will jump from their horses, but they will sink into the earth also. Then you can do as you desire with them. Now, you must know this, that all the soldiers and that race will be dead. There will be only five thousand of them left living on earth. My friends and relations, this is straight and true.[16]

U.S. Army leaders feared that the Ghost Dance would lead to new Indian uprisings, so soldiers began arresting Ghost Dance leaders. The climax of this campaign occurred in late

December 1890, when U.S. cavalry units surrounded a group of Sioux, including a number of Ghost Dancers, along Wounded Knee Creek in South Dakota. During the attempt to arrest the Indians, a weapon went off, initiating a killing spree in which the soldiers fired repeatedly at unarmed men, women, and children. A few minutes later, 153 Indians, including the group's leader, Chief Big Foot, lay dead.

A Sense of Shame and Outrage

Overall, Native Americans had suffered more than just defeat by the United States between the 1770s and the tragedy at Wounded Knee in 1890. In successfully fulfilling its manifest destiny to gain control of the continent, white American civilization decimated an entire way of life. White hunters destroyed almost all of the great buffalo herds on which the Plains Indians had substantially based their livings. And tens of thousands of Indians across the continent died of white diseases (brought to the New World from the Old), including measles, smallpox, and cholera.

Forced removal and relocation also took its toll. At the time that the Ghost Dance made its pitiful appearance, virtually all American Indians were confined on reservations in various parts of the country. White officials restricted the reservation Indians' freedom of movement, forbade them to govern themselves, and curtailed their religious freedom. U.S. officials could and often did arrest traditional tribal leaders and healers, often without just cause, while allowing Christian missionaries to roam freely on the reservations, attempting to convert Indians to white beliefs and ways.

Meanwhile, in 1887 Congress passed the General Allotment Act (or Dawes Act). This bill partitioned the reservations into individual parcels in an attempt to transform the Indians into homesteaders in the white tradition. But the bill also allowed the government to sell off "surplus tracts" to white settlers, which caused many reservations steadily to shrink. By 1934, when the Indian Reorganization Act put a stop to this process, and also for the first time allowed Indians to form their own reservation governments, reservation landholdings had fallen from 138 million to 48 million acres.

For many decades, the vast majority of Indians living on the remaining reservation lands suffered from the cruel effects of white racism, inferior educational and health care facilities, and extreme, grinding poverty.

In short, white Americans, zealous for land and natural resources and confident in their supposed racial and cultural superiority, conquered the native inhabitants of the continental United States as completely as any people has ever conquered another. Today, most white Americans view this conquest with a sense of horror, shame, and regret. "Whereas Indian culture creates a sense of wonder," comments Carl Waldman, an authority on Native American history,

> the historical destruction of that culture creates a sense of outrage. . . . For many of the early white historians . . . Indians were an obstacle to manifest destiny, a menace to peaceful white expansion, and perpetrators of frontier violence. That long-standing bias in turn fed the popular conception of Indians as villains, with settlers as victims, and frontiersmen, soldiers, and cowboys as heroes. . . . [However,] the Indian wars are now generally interpreted as wars of native resistance. And since Indians were generally protecting their people, culture and lands from invasion and exploitation from outsiders . . . Indian violence is now regarded in hindsight more sympathetically than white violence. Further Indian justification can be argued because the specific causes of uprisings were often the trickery of white traders, the forced sale of Indian lands, forced labor or enslavement of Indians, the suppression of Indian culture, and the violation of treaties by whites . . . all understandable grievances.

Waldman pointedly and poignantly adds, "Given all that Indian culture and philosophy have to offer modern humanity . . . many perhaps would like to rewrite history with the Indians having a greater hold on human destiny."[17]

Notes

1. John Tebbel and Keith Jennison, *The American Indian Wars*. New York: Harper and Brothers, 1960, pp. 1–2.

2. From a narrative by Henry Brackenridge (originally published in the 1780s in

Freeman's Journal), quoted in Wilcomb E. Washburn, ed., *The Indian and the White Man*. Garden City, NY: Doubleday, 1964, p. 116.

3. Quoted in Washburn, *The Indian and the White Man*, p. 210.

4. *The Winning of the West* (1889–1896), quoted in Edward H. Spicer, *A Short History of the Indians of the United States*. New York: D. Van Nostrand, 1969, pp. 237–39.

5. A.A. Lipscomb and A.E. Bergh, eds., *The Writings of Thomas Jefferson*. 20 vols. Washington, DC: Thomas Jefferson Memorial Association of U.S., 1903, vol. 10, p. 369.

6. Stephen E. Ambrose, *Undaunted Courage: Meriwether Lewis, Thomas Jefferson, and the Opening of the American West*. New York: Simon and Schuster, 1996, p. 337.

7. Quoted in Frederick W. Turner, ed., *The Portable North American Indian Reader*. New York: Viking Press, 1974, p. 247.

8. Quoted in Turner, *Reader*, p. 246.

9. Quoted in Turner, *Reader*, pp. 249–50.

10. Quoted in John Ehle, *Trail of Tears: The Rise and Fall of the Cherokee Nation*. New York: Doubleday, 1988, pp. 357–58.

11. In this small (forty-square-mile), dry, and unproductive area known as Bosque Redondo, the Navajo were expected to learn and adopt white ways and ideas, including Christianity. But this experiment in changing Indians into something they were not and could never become failed miserably. Conditions at Bosque Redondo became so deplorable that local white officials called for a government investigation. In 1868, the Navajo were allowed to return to their former lands, now greatly reduced in size, astride the New Mexico–Arizona border, which became their permanent reservation. For the complete story, see Peter Iverson, *The Navajo Nation*. Albuquerque: University of New Mexico Press, 1981.

12. Tom Holm, "Wars: 1850–1900," in Frederick E. Hoxie, ed., *Encyclopedia of North American Indians*. Boston: Houghton Mifflin, 1996, p. 673.

13. See William O. Taylor, *With Custer on the Little Bighorn*. New York: Viking, 1996.

14. Quoted in Edgar I. Stewart, *Custer's Luck*. Norman: University of Oklahoma Press, 1955, p. 459.

15. Quoted in Dee Brown, *Bury My Heart at Wounded Knee: An Indian History of the American West*. New York: Holt, Rinehart and Winston, 1970, p. 296.

16. Quoted in Spicer, *Short History of the Indians*, pp. 282–83.

17. Carl Waldman, *Atlas of the North American Indian*. New York: Facts On File, 1985, pp. 86–88.

Chapter 1

Different Cultures with Different Visions

Cultural Differences Lead to Misconceptions and Conflict

Alvin M. Josephy Jr.

This informative overview of the initial fundamental cultural differences between American whites and Indians is by Alvin M. Josephy Jr., a noted scholar of Indian culture and history. The two races, says Josephy, came from very different social and intellectual traditions and did not agree about religion, economic values, land ownership, the work ethic, and other basic cultural mores. Inevitably, he explains, these differences, accentuated by white feelings of superiority, led to unfair and unflattering stereotyping of Indians by whites and eventually to interracial friction, misunderstandings, and violence between the two races.

The beliefs, ways of life, and roles of the American Indians are interwoven so intimately with the cultures and histories of all the modern nations of the Americas that no civilization of the Western Hemisphere can be fully understood without knowledge and appreciation of them. And yet, from the time of the Europeans' first meeting with the Indians in 1492 until today, the Indian has been a familiar but little known—and, indeed, often an unreal—person to the non-Indian. What has been known about him, moreover, frequently has been superficial, distorted, or false.

Derivation of the Term "Indian"

What the white man calls him is itself the result of an error. When Christopher Columbus reached the New World, he had no idea that a land mass lay between Europe and Asia; the islands at which he touched he thought were those known at

Reprinted from chapter one of *The Indian Heritage of America*, by Alvin M. Josephy Jr. (New York: Knopf, 1968). Copyright 1968 by Alvin M. Josephy Jr. Reprinted by permission of the author.

the time as the Indies, which lay off the coast of Asia, and the people he found on them he called *los Indios*, the people of the Indies, or the Indians. Other early navigators and chroniclers used the same name mistakenly for the various peoples they met at the end of each westward voyage, and by the time the Europeans discovered their error and realized that they were still far from Asia, it was too late. The name had taken hold as a general term of reference for all the inhabitants of the newly found lands of the Western Hemisphere.

Condemning What They Did Not Understand

Errors of far greater significance—and seriousness— stemmed from fundamental cultural differences between Indians and non-Indians. Deeply imbedded in the cultural make-up of the white man with a European background were the accumulated experiences of the Judeo-Christian spiritual tradition, the heritages of the ancient civilizations of the Near East, Greece, and Rome, and the various political, social, and economic systems of western Europe. The Indians did not share any of these, but, on their part, were the inheritors of totally different traditions and ways of life, many of them rooted in Asia, some of them thousands of years old, and all as thoroughly a part of Indian societies as European ways were a part of the white man's culture.

Meeting peoples with such different backgrounds led white men to endless misconceptions. Beginning with Columbus, the whites, with rare exceptions, observed and judged natives of the Americas from their own European points of view, failing consistently to grasp the truths and realities of the Indians themselves or their backgrounds and cultures. In the early years of the sixteenth century educated whites, steeped in the theological teachings of Europe, argued learnedly about whether or not Indians were humans with souls, whether they, too, derived from Adam and Eve (and were therefore sinful like the rest of mankind), or whether they were a previously unknown subhuman species. Other Europeans spent long years puzzling on the origin of the Indians and developing evidence that they were Egyptians, Chinese, descendants of one of the Lost Tribes of Israel, Welshmen, or even the survivors of civilizations that had once flourished on lost continents in the Atlantic and Pacific oceans.

In the lands of the New World, white men who came in contact with Indians viewed Indian cultures solely in terms that were familiar to themselves, and ignored or condemned what they did not understand. Indian leaders were talked of as "princes" and "kings"; spiritual guides and curers were called wizards, witch doctors, and medicine men, and all were equated as practitioners of sorcery; Indian societies generally—refined and sophisticated though some of them might be—were termed savage and barbaric, often only because they were strange, different, and not understood by the whites.

Many of the differences brought friction and, on both continents, fierce, interracial war. Conflicts resulted from misconceptions of the nature of Indian societies, the limits of authority of Indian leaders, and the non-hostile motives of certain Indian traits. Differing concepts concerning individual and group use of land and the private ownership of land were at the heart of numerous struggles, as were misunderstandings over the intentions of Indians whose actions were judged according to the patterns of white men's behavior rather than those of the Indians.

The Natural Man

Through the years, the white man's popular conception of the Indian often crystallized into unrealistic or unjust images. Sometimes they were based on the tales of adventurers and travelers, who wove myths freely into their accounts, and sometimes they were reflections of the passions and fears stirred by the conflicts between the two races. Described by early writers as a race of happy people who lived close to nature, the Indians of the New World were first envisioned by many Europeans as innocent, childlike persons, spending their time in dancing and equally pleasurable pursuits. From this image in time sprang [French philosopher] Jean Jacques Rousseau's vision of the natural man, as well as arguments of liberal philosophers in Europe who influenced revolutionary movements, including those of the United

States and France, with comparisons between the lot of Europeans "in chains" and Indians who lived lives of freedom.

This idealistic version of the Indian as a symbol of the naturally free man persisted into the nineteenth century, sometimes being advanced by admiring observers like the artist George Catlin who visited many tribes and found much to admire in their ways of life, but generally being accepted only by persons who had no firsthand contact with Indians. On each frontier, beginning along the Atlantic coast, settlers who locked in conflict with Indians quickly conceived of them as bloodthirsty savages, intent on murder, scalping, and pillage. As the frontier moved west, and the Indian menace vanished from the eastern seaboard, generations that did not know Indian conflict at firsthand again thought of the native American in more tolerant terms. [American novelist] James Fenimore Cooper's version of the Noble Red Man helped gain sympathy among easterners for Indians who were hard pressed by the whites elsewhere. Thus, throughout much of the nineteenth century people in the northeastern cities often gave support to movements for justice for the southern and western tribes.

But as long as conflicts continued, the border settlers . . . echoed the sentiment that "the only good Indian is a dead Indian." Only with the defeat of tribes did that point of view change—and then, inevitably, it was succeeded by still another image, which also moved from one border to another as settlers took over lands from which they had dispossessed the natives. It was the cruel conception of the Whisky Indian, the destroyed and impoverished survivor who had lost his home, tribal life, means of sustenance, and cultural standards, and lacking motivation—and often even the will to live—sought escape in alcohol. Unfeeling whites, failing to recognize the causes of the Indians' degradation, forgot their past power, pride, and dignity, and regarded them as weak and contemptuous people.

Whites Deceived About Indians

Only rarely did astute observers try to understand Indian life and depict Indians realistically. One of them, Edwin T. Denig, an American fur trader living among still-unconquered tribes on the upper Missouri River during the first half of the nineteenth century, wrote angrily on the white man's lack of knowledge about Indians at that time.

It would be well for the public if everyone who undertook to write a book was thoroughly acquainted with the subject of which he treats. . . . This is particularly the case in most of the works purporting to describe the actual life and intellectual capacity of the Indians of North America; much evil has been the consequence of error thus introduced, bad feelings engendered, and unwise legislation enforced, which will continue until our rulers are enlightened as to the real state of their Government, character, organization, manners and customs, and social position . . . a hastily collected and ill-digested mass of information form the basis of works by which the public is deceived as to the real state of the Indians. Even foreigners who have possibly passed a winter at some of the trading posts in the country, seen an Indian dance or two or a buffalo chase, return home, enlighten Europe if not America with regard to Indian character; which is only the product of their own brains and takes its color from the peculiar nature of that organ. Hence we find two sets of writers both equally wrong, one setting forth the Indians as a noble, generous, and chivalrous race far above the standard of Europeans, the other representing them below the level of brute creation.

A Totally Alien Way of Life?

It might be assumed that much has changed since the time when Denig wrote. But despite vast study by scientists and a voluminous literature of modern knowledge about Indians, still common are ignorance and misconceptions, many of them resulting from the white man's continuing inability to regard Indians save from his own European-based point of view. Today most Indians . . . have been conquered and enfolded within the conquerors' own cultures; but the span of time since the various phases of the conquest ended has been short, and numerous Indians still cling to traits that are centuries, if not millennia, old and cannot be quickly shed.

Many Indians, for instance, still do not understand or cannot accept the concept of private ownership of land; many do not understand the need to save for the future, a fundamental requirement of the economies of their conquerors; many find it difficult, if not impossible so far, to substitute individual competitiveness for group feeling; many do not see the necessity for working the year-round if they can provide for their families by six months of work, or the reason for cutting the earth-mother with a plow and farming if they can still hunt, fish, and dig roots. Many yet feel a sacred attachment to the land and a reverence for nature that is incomprehensible to most whites. Many, though Christian, find repugnance in the idea that man possesses dominion over the birds and beasts, and believe still that man is brother to all else that is living.

Such ideas, among a multitude that continue to hold numerous Indians apart from non-Indians, are either unrecognized or frowned upon by most whites today. Those who are aware of them are more often than not irritated by their persistence, yet the stubbornness of the white critics' own culture to survive, if a totally alien way of life, like that of the Chinese Communists, were to be forced upon them, would be understood.

White Stereotypes of Indians

More common among most whites are the false understandings and images which they retain about Indians. For many, the moving pictures, television, and comic strips have firmly established a stereotype as the true portrait of all Indians: the dour, stoic, warbonneted Plains Indian. He is a warrior, he has no humor unless it is that of an incongruous and farcical type, and his language is full of "hows," "ughs," and words that end in "um." Only rarely in the popular media of communications is it hinted that Indians, too, were, and are, all kinds of real, living persons like any others and that they included peace-loving wise men, mothers who cried for the safety of their children, young men who sang songs of love and courted maidens, dullards, statesmen, cowards, and patriots. Today there are college-trained Indians, researchers, business and professional men and women, jurists, ranchers, teachers, and political office holders. Yet so enduring is the stereotype that many a non-Indian, especially if he lives in an area where Indians are not commonly seen, expects any American Indian he meets to wear a feathered headdress. When he sees the Indian in a conventional business suit instead, he is disappointed!

Not All One People

If Indians themselves are still about as real as wooden sticks to many non-Indians, the facts concerning their present-day status in the societies of the Americas are even less known. Again, stereotypes, like those of "the oil-rich Indian" or "the coddled ward of Uncle Sam" frequently obscure the truth. A few Indians have become wealthy, but most of them know poverty, ill health, and barren, wasted existences. Some have received higher education, but many are poorly educated or not educated at all. Some are happily assimilated in the white man's societies; others are in various stages of acculturation, and many are not assimilated and do not wish to be anything but Indian. In the United States, in addition, it often comes as a surprise to many otherwise well informed whites to learn that the Indians are citizens and have the right to vote; that reservations are not concentration camps but are all the lands that were left to the Indians, and that are still being guarded by them as homes from which they can come and go in freedom; that the special treaty rights that they possess and that make them a unique minority in the nation are payments and guarantees given them for land they sold to the non-Indian people of the United States; that Indians pay state and federal taxes like all other citizens, save where treaties, agreements, or statutes have exempted them; and that, far from being on the way to extinction, the Indian population is increasing rapidly.

Finally, there are facts that should be obvious to everyone after five hundred years but are not, possibly because Columbus's name for them, Indians, is to this day understood by many to refer to a single people. Despite the still commonly asked question, "Do you speak Indian?" there is neither a single Indian people nor a single Indian language, but many different peoples, with different racial characteristics, different cultures, and different languages. From Alaska to Cape Horn, in fact, the Indians of the Americas are as different from each other as are Spaniards, Scots, and Poles—and, in many cases . . . they are even more different.

Why White Americans Had Difficulty Understanding Indian Religion

George E. Tinker

Religious beliefs constituted (and still constitute) one of the major examples of cultural difference separating whites and Native Americans. In this essay, George E. Tinker, a teacher at the Iliff School of Theology in Denver and a member of the Osage tribe, summarizes basic Indian religious conceptions and how whites, whom he refers to as Euro-Americans, found them strange and often inexplicable. He points out, for instance, how Indians tended to identify with specific powerfully spiritual places, usually on or near their ancestral lands. Having to leave these sacred places behind made white removal and relocation policies especially traumatic and disorienting for Indians. By contrast, white Christians more often identified with spiritual days or time periods, such as Sunday or Lent. The complexity and mysteriousness of Native American religious beliefs, as viewed through white eyes, was one of the major reasons for tensions and fighting between the two races.

The phenomena referred to by the term *Native American religions* pose an interesting and complex problem of description and interpretation—one that has consistently captured the imagination of European immigrant peoples. These phenomena have been misunderstood, maligned, romanticized, and misappropriated. In almost every case the authoritative and definitive analyses of particular Native American religious traditions have been written by non-Indians, and thus

Excerpted from "Religion," by George E. Tinker, from *Encyclopedia of North American Indians*, edited by Frederick E. Hoxie. Copyright ©1996 by Houghton Mifflin Company. Reprinted by permission of Houghton Mifflin Company. All rights reserved.

nonadherents, who lacked any lifelong experiential basis for their analyses. It seems that now, at the end of the twentieth century, deeply held Indian traditions and beliefs have been politicized—on the one hand by academic experts, and on the other by New Age aficionados [devotees] who have mistakenly seen Indian spirituality as a new trade commodity. It has become increasingly clear that those phenomena we call Native American religions were and are yet today very complex socially and philosophically and are therefore not easily represented or described by means of either popular interpretation or the critical categories of academic analysis, especially when those categories have been constructed in a cultural context alien to the traditions themselves.

The Two "Grand Divisions"

Most adherents to traditional American Indian ways characteristically deny that their people ever engaged in any religion at all. Rather, these spokespeople insist, their whole culture and social structure was and still is infused with a spirituality that cannot be separated from the rest of the community's life at any point. The Green Corn Ceremony, the Snake Dance, kachinas, the Sun Dance, sweat-lodge ceremonies, and the sacred pipe are not specifically religious constructs of various tribes but rather represent specific ceremonial aspects of a world that includes countless ceremonies in any given tribal context, ceremonies performed by whole communities, clans, families, or individuals on a daily, periodic, seasonal, or occasional basis. Whereas outsiders may identify a single ritual as the "religion" of a particular people, the people themselves will likely see that ceremony as merely an extension of their day-to-day existence, all parts of which are experienced within ceremonial parameters and should be seen as "religious."

For instance, among the *Ni U Konska* (Osages), what ethnographers would classify as "religion" pervades even the habitual acts of sleeping and putting on shoes. All the ceremonies and prayers of the Osages reflect the principle of the simultaneous duality and unity of all existence. Prayers commonly begin with an address to the Wakonda Above and the

Wakonda Below (manifested in Sky and Earth, respectively), the two great fructifying forces of the universe. This principle is mirrored in the architectural structure of Osage towns and in the marriage customs of the people. Each Osage town was divided by an east-west road into two "grand divisions" representing Sky and Earth. Just as Osages perceived the necessity of these two forces coming together in order for life to be sustained, so too they saw the two grand divisions of the people as sustaining the life of the whole. To insure that the principle of spiritual and political unity in this duality would be maintained, Osages were mandated by social custom to marry someone from the other grand division. To further enforce this religious sense of wholeness, members of each of the two grand divisions developed distinct personal habits that helped remind them of their own part in the communal whole. For instance, those from the Honga grand division customarily slept on their right side and put on the right shoe first, whereas those from the Tsizhu grand division functioned in the opposite manner. As a result, even in sleep the two divisions performed a religious act that maintained their unity in duality as they lay facing each other across the road that divided the community.

Community-Based Traditions

Thus the social structures and cultural traditions of American Indian peoples are infused with a spirituality that cannot be separated from, say, picking corn or tanning hides, hunting game or making war. Nearly every human act was accompanied by attention to religious details, sometimes out of practiced habit and sometimes with more specific ceremony. In the Northwest, harvesting cedar bark would be accompanied by prayer and ceremony, just as killing a buffalo required ceremonial actions and words dictated by the particularities of tribal nation, language, and culture. Among the Osages the spiritual principle of respect for life dictated that the decision to go to war against another people usually required an eleven-day ceremony—allowing time to reconsider one's decision and to consecrate the lives that might be lost as a result of it. Because to be successful the hunt required acts of violence, it was also considered a type of war. Hence the semiannual community buffalo hunt, functioning on the same general principle of respect for life, also required a ceremony—one that was in all respects nearly identical to the War Ceremony.

Perhaps the most distinctive aspect of American Indian religious traditions is the extent to which they are wholly community based and have no real meaning outside of the specific community in which the acts are regularly performed, stories told, songs sung, and ceremonies conducted. [Noted Native American writer] Vine Deloria, Jr., described the communitarian foundations of American Indian existence in his 1973 book *God Is Red*, his point being that ceremonies are engaged in not primarily for personal benefit but rather for the benefit of an entire community or nation. The most common saying one hears during the Lakota Sun Dance is "That the people might live!" This sentiment becomes the overriding reason for and purpose of this ceremony. Likewise, violations of the sacred become threatening to the whole community and not merely to the one who commits the error. The communitarian nature of Indian ceremonies represents a key distinction between Native American religious traditions and modern Euro-American New Age spirituality, with its emphasis on radical individualism.

White Attitudes Disruptive

Some would argue that the so-called vision quest is evidence of the quintessential individualism of Plains Indian peoples. However, just the opposite can be argued, because in Plains cultures the individual is always in symbiotic relationship with the community. This ceremony involves personal sacrifice: rigorous fasting (no food or liquids) and prayer over several days (typically four to seven) in a location removed from the rest of the community. Yet in a typical rite of vigil or vision quest, the community or some part of the community assists the individual in preparing for the ceremony and then prays constantly on behalf of the individual throughout the ceremony. Thus by engaging in this ceremony, the individual acts on behalf of and for the good of the whole community. Even when an individual seeks personal power or assistance through such a ceremony, he or she is doing so for the ultimate benefit of the community.

"We Never Quarrel About Religion"

That Indians and whites had great difficulty conceptualizing and understanding each other's religions is well illustrated in this excerpt from a conversation between a Seneca chief and a Boston missionary in 1805. The chief's remarks show that he found white beliefs just as strange and illogical as whites found Indian beliefs.
"*Brother;* Continue to listen.

"You say that you are sent to instruct us how to worship the Great Spirit agreeably to his mind, and, if we do not take hold of the religion which you white people teach, we shall be unhappy hereafter. You say that you are right and we are lost. How do we know this to be true? We understand that your religion is written in a book. If it was intended for us as well as you, why has not the Great Spirit given to us, and not only to us, but why did he not give to our forefathers, the knowledge of that book, with the means of understanding it rightly? We only know what you tell us about it. How shall we know when to believe, being so often deceived by the white people?

"*Brother;* You say there is but one way to worship and serve the Great Spirit. If there is but one religion; why do you white people differ so much about it? Why not all agreed, as you can all read the book?

"*Brother;* We do not understand these things.

"We are told that your religion was given to your forefathers, and has been handed down from father to son. We also have a religion, which was given to our forefathers, and has been handed down to us their children. We worship in that way. It teaches us to be thankful for all the favors we receive; to love each other, and to be united. We never quarrel about religion."

Quoted in Wilcomb E. Washburn, ed., *The Indian and the White Man.* Garden City, NY: Doubleday, 1964, pp. 212–13.

Unfortunately, the traditional symbiotic relationship between the individual and the community, exemplified in ceremonies such as the vision quest, has become severely distorted as a shift in Euro-American cultural values has begun
to encourage the adoption and practice of Indian spirituality
by the general population no matter how disruptive this may
be to Indian communities. The resulting incursion of Euro-
American practitioners, who are not a part of the community
in which the ceremony has traditionally been practiced,
brings a Western, individualistic frame of reference to the
ceremony that violates the communitarian cultural values of
Indian peoples. The key concern for Indian people in preserving the authenticity and healthy functioning of the relationship between the individual and the community is the
question of accountability: one must be able to identify what
spiritual and sociopolitical community can rightly make
claims on one's spiritual strength. In the Indian worldview,
this community—this legitimate source of identity—is intimately linked to, and derives directly from, the significance
of spatiality, of space and place.

Space Versus Time

In *God Is Red* Deloria clearly identified and described another characteristic feature of American Indian religious traditions: spatiality. Indian ceremonial life and all of Indian existence are rooted in a profound notion of space and place.
The spatial layout for any ceremony takes on paramount importance. As with the structure of the Osage village, most
Osage ceremonials are structured around a north-south,
Sky-Earth division. In a similar manner, the structure for a
Green Corn Ceremony, the subterranean location of a kiva,
the design of a sweat lodge, or the direction one turns in a
pipe ceremony all have tribally specific cosmic representa-
tional value that reflects the spiritual relationship of a particular people with the spatial world around them. This understanding of the importance of spatiality also emerges in
the longstanding identification of places that are known to a
tribe to be particularly powerful spiritually. For most Indian
communities, there are one or more such places that they

have long identified as powerful: the Black Hills for the Sioux Nation; Blue Lake for Taos Pueblo; Mount Graham for the San Carlos Apaches; the mountains that mark the territorial boundaries of any pueblo—to mention but a few examples.

Indian peoples, then, tend to locate sacred power spatially—in terms of places or in terms of spatial configuration. This is in stark contrast to European and Euro-American religious traditions, which tend to express spirituality in terms of time: a regular hour on Sundays and a seasonal liturgical calendar that has become more and more distanced from any sense of the actual flow of seasons in particular places and is therefore both more abstract and more portable than Native American traditions. In the Southern Hemisphere, for instance, Christians celebrate Lent (named for springtime and the lengthening of the days) and Easter during the antipodean autumn. It would be an exaggeration to argue that Indian peoples have no sense of time or that Europeans have no sense of space. Rather, spatiality is a dominant category of existence for Native Americans whereas time is a subordinate category. Just the opposite is generally true for European peoples.

All the World Alive

The identification of places of particular spiritual power points to yet another important aspect of Indian religious traditions: these places are experienced as powerful because they are experienced as alive. Not only are they sentient; they are intelligent manifestations of what Native Americans call the Sacred Mystery or the Sacred Power. The Sacred Mystery, sometimes simplistically and badly translated as "the Great Spirit," is typically experienced first of all as a great unknown. Yet this unknown becomes known as it manifests itself to humans spatially: as the Mystery Above and Mystery Below; as the Mystery (or Powers) of the Four Directions; as the Sacred Mystery in its self-manifestation in a particular place, in a particular occurrence, in an astronomical constellation, or in an artifact such as a feather. All of the created world is, in turn, seen as alive, sentient, and filled with spiritual power, including each human being. The sense of the interrelationship of all of creation—of all two-legged, four-legged, wingeds, and other living, moving things (from fish and rivers to rocks, trees and mountains)—may be the most important contribution Indian peoples have made to the science and spirituality of the modern world.

Less Advanced Economy and Technology Placed Indians at a Disadvantage

Arrell M. Gibson

In this informative tract, University of Oklahoma scholar
Arrell M. Gibson summarizes the original Native American economy of the region that eventually became the
United States. She explains that this largely simple, subsistence economy was based on a combination of agriculture and hunting and gathering techniques (as opposed to
the economy of the United States, which was based on
both agriculture and rapidly developing industry). Then
she makes the crucial observation that the Indians lacked
certain technological innovations that might have allowed
them to meet encroaching white settlers and soldiers on
equal terms and perhaps keep them at bay. The Native
American failure to make practical applications of the
wheel and to develop advanced metallurgy, for instance,
put them at a fatal disadvantage; for whites possessed these
things and therefore had the technological edge in both
warfare and the production of vital goods and supplies.

That the area later embraced by the United States was in the
seventeenth century a virgin land to be occupied by intrepid
Anglo-American pioneers is a myth. Peoples from Asia had
pioneered this land perhaps as many as 50,000 years earlier.
By 1500 the descendants of these pioneers were distributed
in tribal clusters from the Atlantic to the Pacific, from the
Great Lakes to the Rio Grande. They had occupied the land,
learned its secrets, and formulated techniques to exploit its
abundant resources at a rate sufficient to support themselves

at a level of at least minimum comfort.

The character of the Native American economy, the manner in which the Indians supported themselves, was strongly influenced by environmental conditions. And in turn, their particular economies determined the social models, religion, and political systems adopted by each tribe. Whenever environmental conditions permitted, Native Americans practiced agriculture, although they were never entirely dependent upon it for subsistence, mixing crop production with hunting, fishing, gathering, and trade. Where agriculture was impractical, they sustained themselves in the style of the Archaic—intensive exploitation of the environment through hunting, fishing and gathering. Certain staples dominated the economy of various tribal territories. In the humid, well-watered East corn was supreme. Tribes in the Great Lakes area gathered wild rice. For the Great Plains hunters the buffalo was the staple. Corn, produced by irrigated agriculture, sustained the economy of the desert Southwest. The acorn supported a surprisingly large population in California. Salmon was the mainstay for the tribes of the Pacific Northwest, both on the coast and in the interior plateau. . . .

Hunting and Gathering

Aborigines in the lower Mississippi Valley best exemplify the Native American's talent for coordinating the ancient skills of hunting and gathering with agriculture to establish the economic foundations for one of North America's highest Indian civilizations. These Native Americans obtained food, shelter, clothing, and other needs from nature's bounty by hunting and gathering, agriculture, some trade with other tribes, and plunder from wars with neighbors.

There was a rather precise division of labor, based on sex, among these Indians. Men protected their households and communities, campaigned against enemy nations, provided meat for their households by hunting and fishing, performed tribal political and religious duties, and were artisans for certain crafts, particularly tools and weapons. Women managed households, provided meals and clothing for their families, gathered foods from nature, dominated certain crafts including weaving, and tended the crops.

The male was first and foremost a warrior and a hunter. He mixed his invocation of spirit power and supernatural approval for success on the game trails with the familiar skills of tracking, trapping, and using decoys and calls. The largest hunt occurred in the autumn. If successful, hunters turned most of their skins and smoked meat over to their households although they customarily set aside a portion for feasts and for food gifts to old people in the village. Young boys hunted wild turkeys and other small game near the villages as a part of their training.

The basic meat in the economy of the lower Mississippi tribes was the deer and bear, plus the bison when hunting parties went to the prairies. Deer was the favorite; its flesh was eaten fresh or dried and smoked for winter use. Its skin served as the principal material for clothing. Antler tips were often used as arrow points, and dried deer sinew and entrails were twisted and used for bowstrings and thread for sewing and weaving fishnets. Indian women used deer brains for softening and tanning skins. The bear ranked next in usefulness. Women fashioned heavy winter robes and bed coverings from bearskins. The rough hide was made into strong moccasins and hunting boots, and dried bear gut was a favorite with the warriors as bowstring material. They pierced bear claws for ornaments and necklaces. An important product from the bear was oil. Women took slabs of fat from the carcass and rendered them over fires, producing a clear oil which they mixed with sassafras and wild cinnamon and stored in large earthen jars. Indians used bear oil as cooking oil, as a hair dressing, and as a body rub for common complaints.

At certain seasons, fish was a popular food. Men made substances to drug fish from devil's shoestring, buckeye, and crushed green walnut hulls which they cast into deep holes in the rivers and creeks near their villages. When the drugged catfish, drum, and bass surfaced, the fishermen caught them by hand, speared them, or retrieved them with arrows fitted with a special barb and a hand line; they also placed creels, weirs, and nets on the edge of deep holes and in the shallows of rivers to trap fish.

In season, women and children gathered wild onions, grapes, plums, persimmons, mulberries, strawberries, and blackberries, as well as walnuts, chestnuts, pecans, acorns, and hickory nuts. They dried plums and grapes into primitive prunes and raisins and pressed dried persimmons into cakes. Boiled sassafras roots made a popular tea. The Indians gathered salt from local licks and springs, and robbed bee trees for honey which they used for sweetening. They felled the bee tree and placed the comb and thick, sweet liquid in a sewed deerskin container.

Agriculture and Crafts

Agriculture matched hunting and gathering in importance in their economy. Public farms and household gardens were planted near the villages on meadow and prairie plots and cleared tracts in the timber. Workers cleared forest patches by deadening trees. They killed each tree by girdling, cutting a circle through the tree bark with notched stone axes; then they burned it, using saplings and undergrowth as fuel. Corn was the principal crop. Between the grain hills in the corn patches farmers planted melons, pumpkins, squash, sunflowers, beans, peas, and tobacco. Women served green corn as roasting ears and processed ripe corn into porridge, grits, gruel, hominy, and meal for bread. They crushed dried corn kernels with a long-handled pestle in a mortar made from a chunk of hollowed hickory.

These peoples also used many other items in nature to meet their needs for clothing, decoration, household utensils, ceremonial tools, and shelter. Besides chipping stone pieces into projectile points, knives, and axes, they fashioned local clays into pottery vessels for cooking and for storing food and water. They spun thread and yarn for textiles out of the inner bark of the mulberry tree and animal fur. They converted eagle, hawk, and swan feathers into elegant decorative pieces, notably the warrior's mantle. They colored textiles and finely tanned deerskins with a bright yellow dye made from sassafras roots, and red, yellow, and black dyes from sumac. Walnut hulls yielded a rich dark dye used to color baskets and to mix with bear oil to color their hair.

The forests of the lower Mississippi Valley yielded many products useful in their crafts. Large logs were hollowed out by fire; when the charred insides were scraped with clam shells or sharpened stones, the result was river boats. From pine trees they took material for the framework for their houses and made pitch torches. Cane was another important plant for their crafts. They wove cane baskets and mats, used woven cane for house siding, constructed cane fish traps, sieves, and fences, and made blowguns from hollowed cane stems. The hickory tree had a number of uses. Besides using the nuts for food, they split hickory logs into strong, resilient withes or strips and wove house walls and heavy containers. Hickory was an important firewood, and its bark was used to cover shelters. Because of its strength, craftsmen used it to make arrow shafts and bows; in fact, white hickory ranked with black locust as the favorite bow wood. Red hickory was used for making mortars and pestles for grinding grain.

Intertribal Commerce

Economic life was enriched by commerce with other tribes. These Indians counted quantity by tens. Traders exchanged deerskins, Indian slaves, and bear oil sealed in clay urns with merchants from other tribes for special materials required in the construction of war implements; for conch shells, used as ceremonial chalices; and for pearls and sheet copper for making ornaments.

As indicated, women among these Indian nations did most of the household work and labor in the fields. Thus they prized the Indian slaves captured in their tribe's wars. And the women could be expected to urge their men to more fury, more raids, and the taking of more slaves, which changed their own status from laborers to overseers of slave laborers. To prevent escape from bondage, the captors mutilated their slaves' feet by cutting nerves or sinews just above the instep. Thus hobbled, the slaves could work but could not flee.

Warriors labored on the public farms and other civil works, constructed houses, and made tools and implements of war. They spent most of their time on the game trail and warpath or resting from their exertions and watching the women and slaves toil. Europeans condemned these men as slothful. They charged that a male bestirred himself only, as one of them put it, "when the devil is at his arse."

Technological Disadvantages

Native Americans lacked several basic items that would have enhanced their technology, made their dominion over the land less fragile, and made them more of a match for the Europeans. First, they lacked the wheel. Second, Native Americans had no large domesticated animals such as the horse, ox, and cow. And third, they had no knowledge of metallurgy other than hammering sheet copper into tools and gold and silver into ornaments.

Lack of knowledge of the principle of the wheel restricted their technology including land transportation. Dogs pulled sleds and the travois, and slaves acted as porters for moving goods overland. They used water transportation when available, ingeniously developing boats adapted to their environment. The northern tribes developed the bark-covered canoe, its joints and seams waterproofed with pitch. Indians in other parts of North America devised large rafts, dugouts, round hide-covered bull boats, and ocean-going, double-rigged craft with sails. . . . Lack of the wheel also limited their access to labor-saving devices like the pulley.

Native Americans domesticated the dog to guard their settlements, to hunt, [and] to act as a burden bearer with travois poles. . . . Some tribes used dogs for food. They also domesticated the turkey for food and feathers. Tribes of the Pacific Northwest approached domestication when they developed fish farming, stocking streams by depositing salmon eggs at favorable locations.

However, their lack of large domesticated animals and their failure to apply water power to grinding grain and other burdensome tasks made Indians unduly dependent upon human muscle power. And their limited metallurgical knowledge restricted weapon and tool materials to stone, wood, bone, antler, and hammered copper, no match for the iron tools, weapons and cooking utensils of the Europeans.

Attitudes Shaped by Economic Factors

As emphasized earlier, the manner in which Indians supported themselves had a great influence on their religion, social and political system, and lifestyle generally. Time spent obtaining food was a crucial factor in life-style quality. Those groups who spent most of each day searching for food could be expected to have an uncomplicated life-style. The search for food required that they travel great distances for meat, roots, berries, nuts, and fish to sustain themselves. Theirs was a hand-to-mouth existence. Casting over one part of their hunting territory one day, another the next, they developed no sense of specific place or fixed abode.

On the other hand, those tribes that practiced agriculture were sedentary. They occupied fixed territories, residing in villages. Farming was demanding; crops required regular care. Agriculture also generally supported more people than an exclusively hunting-gathering economy. With public management a surplus of grain and other essentials could be produced, collected, stored, and distributed in times of crop failure or other disaster. Specialization of labor, refinement of craft skills, and more intricate division of labor were also possible. More people living close together in each community required a more elaborate, complicated social system and control to regulate individual behavior, to protect the group interest, and to manage effectively the larger human group than were required in the simple hunting-gathering economy.

Manifest Destiny: The U.S. Vision of Expansion

James W. Davidson et al.

To a large degree, Native American civilization was a victim of manifest destiny, the idea that the United States was fated to stretch "from sea to shining sea." As the new nation expanded westward in the late 1700s and early 1800s, it became increasingly clear that the Mississippi River would not be, as many had long pictured it, the permanent boundary between white and Indian lands. Texas, New Mexico, California, Oregon, and other western regions irresistibly beckoned white traders, settlers, and developers. These areas were inhabited not only by Indians, but also by the Spanish-speaking Mexicans, another group white Americans came to view as standing in the way of U.S. expansion. In their recent study of American history, *Nation of Nations*, scholars James W. Davidson, William E. Gienapp, Christine L. Heyrman, Mark H. Lytle, and Michael B. Stoff provide this concise examination of the roots of and beliefs inherent in manifest destiny.

"Make way . . . for the young American Buffalo—he has not yet got land enough," bellowed one American politician in 1844. "We will give him Oregon for his summer shade," Texas "as his winter pasture," and "the use of two oceans—the mighty Pacific and the turbulent Atlantic" to quench his thirst.

In the space of a few years, the United States acquired Texas, California, the lower part of the Oregon Territory, and the lands between the Rockies and California: nearly 1.5 million square miles in all. To many a "young Buffalo," such acquisitions seemed only proper. John L. O'Sullivan, a prominent Democratic editor in New York, struck a responsive chord when he declared that it had become the United States' "manifest destiny to overspread the continent allotted by Providence for the free development of our yearly multiplying millions." The cry of "Manifest Destiny" soon echoed in other editorial pages and in the halls of Congress.

The Roots of Manifest Destiny

Many Americans had long believed that their country had a special, even divine mission. The Protestant version of this conviction could be traced back to John Winthrop, who assured his fellow Puritans that God intended them to build a model "city upon a hill" for the rest of the world to emulate. During the Revolution, many Americans, including the Reverend Ebenezer Baldwin of Danbury, Connecticut, expected that the colonies would one day become "a great and mighty Empire; the largest the World ever saw." [Religious] revivalists . . . spoke similarly of a coming Christian "millennium": a thousand years of peace and prosperity toward which America, by its example, would lead the way.

Manifest Destiny also contained a political component, inherited from the ideology of the Revolution. Baldwin, for example, had argued that the holy American empire would be founded on the "principles of Liberty and Freedom, both civil and religious." In the mid–nineteenth century, future president James Buchanan echoed this dream of a nation "extending the blessings of Christianity and of civil and religious liberty over the whole North American continent." By "civil liberty," he meant a democracy with widespread suffrage, no king or aristocracy, and no established church. In that sense, Manifest Destiny reflected the democratic reforms of the Jacksonian era. But it was a social and economic system, too, that Americans believed should spread around the globe. That system, they argued, encouraged a broad ownership of land, individualism, and the free play of economic opportunity. This doctrine had its self-interested side, of course, for American business interests recognized the value of the fine harbors along the Pacific Coast and hoped to make them American. As Senator Thomas Hart Benton proclaimed, the West was the road to India. By traveling it, a lucrative trade with the Orient would grow and flourish.

Nothing Could Stand in the Way

Finally, underlying other assumptions about Manifest Destiny was a persistent and widespread racism. The same belief in racial superiority that was used to justify Indian removal under Jackson, to uphold slavery in the South, and to excuse segregation in the North also proved handy to defend expansion westward. The United States had a duty to regenerate the backward peoples of America, declared politicians and propagandists. Their reference was not so much to In-

Rapid Strides Beyond the Mississippi

In this speech, made in August 1838 to members of a Baptist church in Buffalo, New York, Maris Bryant Pierce, a member of the Seneca tribe, protests the recent exploitation of his people by white land speculators and the relocation of the tribe to Indian Country. The speech is noteworthy for its recognition of the relentlessness of white expansion, part of what would later be termed the "manifest destiny" of white Americans.

In the first place the white man wants our land; in the next place it is said that the offer for it is liberal; in the next place that we shall be better off to remove from the vicinity of the whites and settle in the neighborhood of our fellow red man, where the woods flock with game, and the streams abound with fishes. . . .

The fact that the whites want our land imposes no obligation on us to sell it, nor does it hold forth an inducement to do so, unless it leads them to offer a price equal in value to us. We neither know nor feel any debt of gratitude which we owe to them, in consequence of their "loving kindness or tender mercies" toward us, that should cause us to make a sacrifice of our property or our interest, to their wonted avarice and which, like the mother of the horse leech, cries give, give, and is never sated. . . . By what mode of calculation or rules of judgment is one or two dollars a liberal offer to us, when many times that sum

dians—who stubbornly refused to assimilate into American society—but to Mexicans, whose Christian nation had its roots in European culture. The Mexican race "must amalgamate and be lost, in the superior vigor of the Anglo-Saxon race," proclaimed O'Sullivan's *Democratic Review*, "or they must utterly perish."

Before 1845 most Americans assumed that expansion would be achieved peacefully. American settlement would spread westward and, when the time was ripe, neighboring provinces, like ripe fruit, would fall into American hands naturally. Neither mountains nor deserts nor (in their eyes) backward cultures could stand in the way. Nor did Ameri-

---

would be only fair to the avarice of the land speculator? Since in us is vested a perfect title to the land, I know not why we may not, when we wish, dispose of it at such prices as we may see fit to agree upon. . . .

"Westward the star of empire takes it away," and whenever that empire is held by the white man, nothing is safe or unmolested or enduring against his avidity for gain. . . . Population is with rapid strides going beyond the Mississippi. . . . And in the process of time, will not our territory there be as subject to the wants of the whites as that which we now occupy is? . . . The proximity of our then situation to that of other and more warlike tribes will expose us to constant harassing by them; and not only this, but the character of those worse than Indians, those *white borderers*, who infest, yes infest, the western border of the white population will annoy us more fatally than even the Indians themselves. Surrounded thus by the natives of the soil, and hunted by such a class of whites, who neither "fear God nor regard man," how shall we be better off there than where we are now? . . .

I need not insult your common sense by endeavoring to show that it is *stupid folly* to suppose that a removal from our present location to the western wilds would improve our condition.

Quoted in Annette Rosenstiel, *Red and White: Indian Views of the White Man, 1492–1982.* New York: Universe Books, 1983, p. 124.

cans doubt in which direction their country's destiny pointed. Texas, New Mexico, Oregon, and California—areas that were sparsely populated and weakly defended—dominated the American imagination. As this destiny became more manifest (to them, at least), Americans became less willing to wait patiently for the fruit to fall.

Indian Unity: A Lost Chance for Survival

Richard White

One of the chief strengths possessed by white Americans during the early years of U.S. westward expansion was widespread unity. By contrast, the many and diverse Indian tribes they encountered more often than not lacked the unity that would have greatly strengthened their resistance to white incursions into their lands. In this essay, Stanford University history professor Richard White briefly examines how, through violence and duplicity, the British and Americans broke up the few true Indian confederations, like those of the Cherokee and Iroquois. Then he traces the attempt made by the legendary Tecumseh and his brother, a religious leader called "the Prophet," to form pan-Indian (or pan-tribal) alliances. As White points out, the failure of Tecumseh's vision of Indian unity ensured the success of the white vision of limitless expansion and the inevitable loss of Indian freedom.

The outbreak of the American Revolution in 1775 seemed to promise a resurgence of the ability of Indians to create a stable political space between competing political powers, but the Revolution proved a disaster for previously powerful Indian confederations. The Cherokees eagerly joined the British cause to drive out the colonials who had been invading their lands, only to face invasion from revolutionary armies that killed their people, destroyed their crops, and burned their towns. Most of the Iroquois also joined the British, only to have their homelands invaded by an American army that methodically cut down their crops and or-

Excerpted from Richard White, "Indian Rebellion," in *The Native Americans: An Illustrated History*, edited by Betty Ballantine and Ian Ballantine (Atlanta: Turner Publishing, 1992). Copyright ©1993 by Turner Publishing, Inc. Reprinted by permission of Richard White.

chards and left their towns in ashes. Most of the Iroquois became refugees dependent on British supplies. The Indians
inflicted huge damage in turn, but the price the Cherokees
and Iroquois paid was so heavy that they never again engaged in direct war with the Americans.

The various Algonquian peoples who joined the British
were militarily victorious north of the Ohio, but they failed
to dislodge the Americans who settled Kentucky. And when
the war ended, they found themselves once more betrayed,
for the British had ceded their homelands to the Americans.
The Americans had received as a British gift lands that their
armies had not been able to conquer. . . .

Pan-Tribalism

In the early nineteenth century two brothers among the
Shawnees, Tecumseh and Tenskwatawa [popularly known as
"the Prophet"], began a movement to reunite and reinvigo-
rate the demoralized peoples north of the Ohio. From the
beginning the movement was pan-tribal and religious, but it
was also a movement that sprang from the middle ground of
more than a century of contact and common life.

Tenskwatawa was one of numerous visionaries, male and
female, among the Shawnees, Delawares, Ottawas, Muskogees, Cherokees, Iroquois, and others during the early nineteenth century who called for a religious renewal among the
tribes. Their calls paralleled, and were in some ways connected with, the First Great Awakening going on among
their American neighbors.

Before his vision, Tenskwatawa had been an inconsequen-
tial drunkard, a figure of ridicule named Lalewethika. Following it, he gave up drinking and took his new name, which
meant "the open door." Although Tenskwatawa's teaching
contained Christian elements, and at least one Shaker leader
recognized the affinities as being close enough to consider
him as being under the same divine inspiration as himself,
Tenskwatawa came to emphasize the differences rather than
the similarities between Indians and whites. His was an Indian religion, an Indian way.

Tenskwatawa and Tecumseh never attained great influence

among the Shawnees, but they gained numerous followers elsewhere and created a series of pan-tribal villages. And to their religious teachings and demands that the Indians renounce drinking and their reliance on white tools and technology, they added an explicit political message: the lands belonged to all Indian peoples in common and no tribe, town, or chief had a right to make a cession. Tecumseh, who gradually

Tecumseh Demands the Restoration of Lost Lands

In this excerpt from his 1811 speech to then U.S. governor (later president) William Henry Harrison, the great Shawnee chief Tecumseh complains that white leaders did not keep their promises to restore lost Indian lands and warns that continued failure to do so will incur the wrath of "all the tribes."

Brother, I was glad to hear your speech. You said that if we could show that the land was sold by people that had no right to sell, you would restore it. Those that did sell did not own it. It was me. These tribes set up a claim, but the tribes with me will not agree with their claim. If the land is not restored to us you will see, when we return to our homes, how it will be settled. We shall have a great council, at which all the tribes will be present, when we shall show to those who sold that they had no right to the claim that they set up, and we will see what will be done to those chiefs that did sell the land to you. I am not alone in this determination; it is the determination of all the warriors and red people that listen to me. I now wish you to listen to me. If you do not, it will appear as if you wished me to kill all the chiefs that sold you the land. I tell you so because I am authorized by all the tribes to do so. I am the head of them all; I am a warrior, and all the warriors will meet together in two or three moons from this; then I will call for those chiefs that sold you the land and shall know what to do with them. If you do not restore the land, you will have a hand in killing them.

Quoted in Edward H. Spicer, *A Short History of the Indians of the United States.* New York: D. Van Nostrand, 1969, p. 269.

took over the leadership of the movement from Tenskwatawa, moved to extend this new confederation beyond the Great Lakes and Ohio River valley and into the south. Capitalizing on another call for religious renewal among the Muskogees, he won a significant following there, but the Cherokees, Chickasaws, and Choctaws largely shunned him.

Tecumseh Seeks British Aid

Tecumseh, for all his stress on Indian unity, knew that his only real chance for success was to secure British backing, and so, despite the two previous betrayals by the British, he once more cultivated a British alliance. Tecumseh regarded war as inevitable, but he sought to delay the advent of fighting until his alliances were complete.

During Tecumseh's absence in the south, however, Tenskwatawa allowed himself to be drawn into a premature fight when, in 1811, an American army illegally invaded Indian lands and marched on Prophetstown at Tippecanoe. He promised his warriors that his spiritual power would render the Americans dead or dying and easy victims, but the soldiers fought back and inflicted significant casualties. Tenskwatawa, who blamed the failure of his medicine on his wife's menstruation, precipitously lost influence, and Tecumseh took sole leadership of the movement.

The fighting had, however, begun and it merged into the War of 1812. Despite initial victories, the end result was defeat both for the Muskogees in the south, and Tecumseh's alliance in the north. When the Americans cut British supply lines on Lake Erie, the British retreated and the victories they and Tecumseh's warriors had won came to naught. On the retreat Tecumseh fell at the Battle of the Thames. His death was a merciful one. He would not live to see his people dispossessed nor to suffer the humiliations of American dictation.

The Loss of Indian Freedom

Tecumseh had never accepted the American claim that American freedom meant Indian freedom, that, in Jefferson's words, the two races would peacefully merge and spread together across the continent. He had recognized that the price of American freedom was the loss of Indian freedom, and that American prosperity would be built on Indian lands. He fought to prevent it; he fought to maintain an older world where the presence of Europeans did not mean the elimination of Indian freedom. He wanted a world where Indian polities were not simply mechanisms for conveying resources to Americans. He failed.

There would, of course, be continued resistance after Tecumseh. But when, following the War of 1812, Great Britain abandoned any further attempts to back independent Indian alliances as a buttress against American expansion, the Indians lost their last real chance to counter the Americans. They would still fight; they would still win military victories, but the chance for ultimate success was gone. And too often the result of resistance was only bloody tragedy.

Chapter 2

Crucial Confrontations Between Indians and Whites

Turning | Points

IN WORLD HISTORY

The First Battles Between the United States and the Indians

John Tebbel and Keith Jennison

During the American Revolution, conflict between the British and Americans had drawn in and devastated the most powerful eastern Indian tribes of the time. Thereafter, the confederation known as the Six Nations, which included the Seneca, Cayuga, Onondaga, Oneida, Mohawk, and Tuscarora, no longer posed a serious threat to white interests. And as the United States emerged as an independent nation free of European control, the line of confrontation between whites and Indians shifted westward to the Ohio Valley. In this excerpt from their masterful survey of the American Indian wars, scholars John Tebbel and Keith Jennison chronicle the initial U.S. Indian policies and battles, in which George Washington, Thomas Jefferson, and General "Mad" Anthony Wayne played key roles. These battles ended in the collapse of Indian resistance in the northwest and set the pattern of misunderstanding, mistrust, and violence that characterized nearly all of the white-Indian confrontations that followed.

The end of the [American] Revolution settled nothing as far as the Indians were concerned. Their grievances against the colonists were as serious as ever, and the fact that General Washington had become President Washington meant little to the red inhabitants of the Ohio Valley, who had lost their faith in white fathers, whether French, British, or native born.

North of the Ohio, in 1790, there existed all the ingredients needed for an explosion. With the Six Nations at last reduced in power, the Miami and Wabash tribes had become

Excerpted from chapter 7 of *The American Indian Wars*, by John Tebbel and Keith Jennison. Copyright ©1960 by John Tebbel and Keith Jennison, renewed ©1988 by John Tebbel. Reprinted by permission of HarperCollins Publishers, Inc.

the chief troublemakers. From the close of the Revolution until October, 1790, it was estimated that these and other tribes had killed, wounded, or taken prisoner nearly 1500 men, women, and children along the Ohio and its tributaries. They had, moreover, stolen at least two thousand horses, and taken other property in the total amount of $50,000.

There were, besides, constant irritating attacks on boats navigating the midwestern rivers. One of the worst of these occurred in April, 1790, when a Major Doughty, en route to visit the Chickasaws on government business, encountered four canoes full of Shawnees and vagabond Cherokees on the Tennessee River. The Indians waved a white flag and were welcomed aboard by the major and his fifteen men, who gave them presents and parted with them an hour later after a friendly conversation.

No sooner had they shoved their canoes off into the river than the Indians turned abruptly and poured a murderous volley into Doughty's boat. The soldiers returned the fire; but before the Indians escaped, eleven of the major's men were dead or wounded

When he heard this news, and similar stories, Washington's patience came to an end. He moved quickly to end what he considered a potentially dangerous situation, now that England and Spain seemed about to go to war, using the Mississippi as their corridor, with all that might mean in the further stirring up of Indian tribes. The President therefore instructed Major General Arthur St. Clair, as Governor of the Northwest Territory, to outfit an expedition against the Indians. St. Clair accordingly summoned 1500 troops at Fort Washington, now Cincinnati, and put them under the command of Brevet Brigadier General Josiah Harmar, who had fought with Pennsylvania troops during the war.

While he was dispensing punishment with one hand, the new President offered friendship with the other. For the first time in the history of the new nation, a band of Indians came to New York, the temporary capital, and visited the President. Washington did not love Indians, but he treated these twenty-nine head men of the Creek nation, accompanied by the noted half-breed leader Alexander McGillivray, with interest and courtesy. Henry Knox conducted the negotiations with them, which resulted in a solemn treaty giving Georgia certain disputed lands but protecting Indian hunting rights in another territory. . . .

Beware of Surprise

By November, the President was increasingly doubtful that Harmar had been the right man to send against the Indians. There was no word from him directly, but disquieting rumors arose at home that he was a heavy drinker. Moreover, Washington learned that St. Clair had sought to reassure the British, who still held their fort at Detroit, that the American force was not marching against them, a piece of information the President concluded correctly that the British would relay immediately to their Indian friends.

This was, in fact, true. Harmar had set out with 300 Federal troops and 1133 militia, sending a force of 600 Kentucky militiamen ahead as a reconnoitering party. These men found themselves following a trail of burned villages as the Indians withdrew slowly, drawing the white men deeper into their territory. When a scouting party of 210 men sought to catch up with them, they turned around, and although outnumbered, frightened the raw militia into precipitate retreat and nearly cut off the regulars who stayed to fight.

Near the destroyed chief village of the Miamis, the Indians turned again and this time attacked Harmar's army with overwhelming strength of their own. More than 150 of the general's men fell dead. The Indian loss was severe enough that they permitted Harmar to retreat with his dead and wounded, a circumstance which led the general in his official report to represent the affair as a victory, although it was a decisive defeat, produced by sheer incompetency. . . .

Arthur St. Clair now took the field, superbly unprepared for what he was commissioned to do. Washington, knowing that St. Clair knew nothing of wilderness fighting, gave him the warning he had given to other embryonic frontier commanders: Beware of surprise. The governor listened and offered a plan of his own. He wanted to establish a post 135 miles north-by-west from Fort Washington, at a place known as the Miami Village, an act intended to serve the double purpose of impressing the Indians and warning the British.

The proposal was adopted, and St. Clair was recommissioned a major general, his wartime rank, which made him the ranking officer of the active army. He was instructed to proceed to the Miami Village with 2000 men and supporting artillery, "establish a strong and permanent military post at that place," and then to "seek the enemy" and "endeavor by all possible means to strike them with great severity."

The whole problem of Indian affairs was a matter for debate in Philadelphia, the new capital. Most people in the government believed that a final settlement with Britain would end the trouble in the Ohio Valley, where the posts still held by the English were a constant annoyance, while the Creeks in the South could be pacified if Spain stopped supplying them with powder and arms from Spanish Florida. Washington's policy was to strengthen existing ties with friendly tribes, and at the same time hammer the resisting nations into submission—the task he had entrusted to St. Clair. Jefferson favored a tougher policy. He believed that the Indians, as a whole, first had to be given a "thorough drubbing," after which "liberal and repeated presents" to them would keep the nations pacified. Washington, who neither loved nor trusted Indians, nevertheless sought a permanent solution in a firm inclusive peace, and the prevention of encroachment on lands that were indubitably the property of the red men.

A Humiliating Defeat

But once more the President had sent the wrong man. St. Clair left Fort Washington on October 3, 1791, and began building small forts on his way to the Miami Village. As he made this slow progress northward, his army began to disintegrate because of the bad planning that had gone into the expedition. Arms and supplies were inadequate, and the militia, which comprised two-thirds of the force, had not been paid its regular monthly rate of three dollars, nor had they bargained to engage in such nonmilitary duties as building forts—on short rations, at that.

The result was a steady trickle of desertions, and departures of militiamen whose terms of enlistment had run out, until only 1400 men remained a month later on the afternoon of November 3, when the army encamped on one of the upper tributaries of the Wabash, a hundred miles north of Fort Washington. By this time St. Clair's incompetence as a commander was painfully evident to the officers accompanying him who had any experience. He would not accept the advice of these officers, and plainly he had no idea of how many Indians were likely to oppose him or of their whereabouts.

If he had known the caliber of the chief who faced him, he would have had good cause to be alarmed. Little Turtle, the Miami leader, whose Indian name was Michikinikwa, was as renowned for his skill in war as he was for his oratory. There were few more important chiefs in the Old Northwest. During the Revolution he had been of considerable help to the British, and the new advance of settlers after it ended had made him all the more hostile to Americans. It was Little Turtle who had brought about Harmar's defeat, and now he confronted St. Clair with a powerful force of Miamis. . . .

The Americans were nearly surrounded and virtually helpless, although the regulars were standing firm and the cannon had been manned. It was an old story. The soldiers stood mostly in ranks and were slaughtered; the Indians fired from cover and were extremely difficult to hit. St. Clair's men fought bravely, and counterattacked with courage when they were ordered, but it was clear that they would be killed and scalped to the last man if they fought it out.

After three hours of combat, this fact was apparent even to St. Clair, and he ordered a retreat. . . . The Indians pursued them for about four miles, then turned away and permitted the 580 survivors to reach safety.

It was a defeat of the most humiliating character. Thirty-nine officers were dead and twenty-one wounded; the total casualties were more than 900 men. The cannon were gone, and so was most of the equipment—abandoned on the field. . . .

No Recourse but War

News of the disaster had trickled back to Philadelphia unofficially by December 8, and next day the town's newspapers carried a story that was substantially correct. St. Clair's official report reached Washington's hands that night. . . .

Washington made no attempt to conceal the bad news from the public. With the honesty that so endeared him to them, he had St. Clair's report published, right down to the last grisly fact. Nevertheless his critics in the press, notably Benjamin Franklin Bache's *General Advertiser*, popularly known as the *Aurora*, began to question the right of Americans to invade Indian lands, especially when it was so expensive in lives and money. . . .

There was pressure for peace with the Indians. Most people appeared to think that would be assured by an army of adequate size, the creation of which was the President's next step. There was a political scramble for the command of this army, and the major general's plum went at last to the impetuous and hotheaded Anthony Wayne . . . one of the Revolution's popular heroes. . . .

While Wayne was slowly building his army in 1792 and 1793, first at Legionville, Pennsylvania, and later near Fort Washington itself, he remained contemptuous of the government's peaceful gestures toward the Indians. Wayne thought no peace was possible. He believed a decisive battle would have to be fought before the Indians of the Northwest Territory gave in, and he was right.

By April, 1793, there was widespread unrest among the tribes, not alone in the Northwest but in the South as well, where Spanish and English agents were at work stirring up trouble. There was increasing hostility among the Creeks, the Seminoles were intermittently on the warpath, and the Chickasaws divided their time between fighting the Creeks and fighting the white settlers. The President made a strong appeal to the Chickasaws for peace, because he believed their help would be needed in case the government found itself involved in a war with the Creeks and Cherokees.

As for the Northwest, the government was ready to make a final attempt at negotiation, and proffer the peace pipe once more to the Ohio tribes at a great council in Sandusky. Commissioners were sent out from Philadelphia for this purpose, and Wayne was instructed to hold himself in readiness for the outcome. Much depended, said Thomas Jefferson, on this "last effort for living in peace with the Indians."

The council was scheduled for the early part of June, but it was July 31 before the chiefs made an appearance at the camp of the commissioners. They immediately demanded that the frontier be established at the Ohio River. . . . That was the old boundary, and there was no chance whatever that the government would agree to it. The commissioners waited two weeks more in the hope that the chiefs would make some other proposal that would at least form the basis for negotiation, but the only further word from the Indians was a repetition of their demand, this time in the form of a written ultimatum. In disgust, the commissioners departed for home.

Thus the great Sandusky conference, from which Jefferson and Washington and Knox had expected so much, in the end was no more than a single brief conversation. There was no recourse now but war—a climactic effort which Washington considered the last and best effort he could make to secure the Northwest frontier.

Panic and Defeat

It was too late for a fall campaign. When Wayne got the news that negotiations had collapsed, he marched his three thousand men from Fort Washington northward, along St. Clair's old route, until he reached the southwest branch of the Maumee, where he built a fort which he named Fort Greenville (or Greeneville), in honor of his old comrade and commander in the Revolution, General Nathanael Greene. There he passed an uneasy winter, beset by desertions, expiration of enlistments, and incipient sedition among his officers.

In spite of these difficulties, Wayne conducted his campaign with masterly skill. He employed delaying tactics which drew Little Turtle into making a strategic error, one of the few in his career. Instead of seizing his chance to isolate Wayne in the spring of 1794, Little Turtle chose to make a sudden attack on the outpost called Fort Recovery, on June 29. It was repulsed with heavy losses, and a good many discouraged Indians went home.

After this failure Little Turtle seems to have realized, with his customary shrewdness, that this time the Indian nations faced a white general of resource and talent, and he foresaw ultimate defeat. He had tried to secure substantial help from the British, but perceived they were ready with urgings and a few supplies while reluctant to commit any men. Consequently, Little Turtle began advocating peace. He used his considerable eloquence in an effort to convince the other chiefs, but they were still boasting of past successes and in no mood to listen. . . .

They took his advice on peacemaking with a chill disdain, and soon Little Turtle had lost his high place in council and his command of the warriors as well. Thus the Indians deprived themselves of the one man who might have saved them from impending defeat. His place was taken by Turkey Foot, a chief of lesser talents. . . .

The two armies met near the rapids of the Maumee at a place called Fallen Timbers, so named because the ground was littered with trees thrown down in a wild confusion, probably caused by a tornado, and affording ideal cover for an army.

These were no inexperienced troops that Wayne brought to the moment of decision. Seeking to avoid the common and fatal error of other wilderness commanders, he had drilled his men skillfully in everything he knew about forest warfare against an Indian enemy until they were virtually perfect in the art.

Arrived at Fallen Timbers, he took a leaf from the Indians' book of warfare and delayed his attack. . . . Then, using the favorite Indian weapon of surprise, Wayne suddenly fell upon the [unprepared Indians]. . . .

The result was panic and flight. Wayne pursued the Indians to the gates of the British fort of Maumee, where the commander had promised them sanctuary in case they were defeated. What bitterness must have gripped the Indians when the commander refused to open the gates. Even as they stood outside the stockade, clamoring for admission, Wayne's men came up and cut them down without mercy.

End of Indian Resistance in the Northwest

It was a disaster for the Indians as bloody as, and far more decisive than, the one that befell St. Clair. Wayne had lost only 38 men, with a hundred or so wounded, while the Indian losses, never revealed as usual, were tragically great. Moreover, the humiliating defeat broke the Indian spirit as nothing else could have done. It was twenty years before the Ohio confederation of tribes recovered from it. To add a final, crushing blow, Wayne burned all of the Indian settlements, destroyed the crops, and laid waste more than five thousand acres of their lands.

Turning to diplomacy, he then convinced the beaten chiefs that their cause was absolutely hopeless, and that they might as well sign a conclusive peace treaty. . . . The Indians could expect no more help of any kind from the British, and without that help, Wayne argued accurately, they could not hope to fight the new American government.

Utterly disheartened, the chiefs agreed. On August 3, 1795, eleven hundred chiefs and warriors gathered with the American peace commissioners at Fort Greenville and signed a peace which ceded a territory comprising all of the present state of Ohio and part of Indiana.

Little Turtle was one of those who signed the treaty, but he took no joy in his vindication. Nor was it the last of the treaties he signed. In time he became a peacemaking go-between for President Harrison, and ultimately a popular Indian hero among the Americans, who were quite ready to forgive his iniquities now that they had his lands. . . .

As he came closer to the white man's ways, his influence with his own people declined, yet he was able to keep the Miamis from joining Tecumseh's confederacy, which was the next chapter in the Indian wars. The chiefs who prophesied that his alliance with the whites would bring him to no good end proved to be correct. In the end, Little Turtle fell victim to a white man's disease, gout, and in spite of treatment from the army surgeon at Fort Wayne, died of it (or more likely, its complications) on July 14, 1812.

The Treaty of Greenville ended Indian resistance in the Old Northwest. The scene of conflict in the long war shifted elsewhere. But at the place where the decisive Battle of Fallen Timbers had been fought, the Indians had the last word—even though it came from the white conqueror. In August 1885, five thousand people from Michigan, Indiana, and Ohio gathered at the battlefield, near Toledo, Ohio, to celebrate Wayne's great victory. They decided that day to erect a monument. Was it a matter of late conscience that impelled them to decree that the monument should arise on the spot where Turkey Foot fell dead? No one knows.

A Last Gamble Against Steep Odds: The Black Hawk War

Robert M. Utley and Wilcomb E. Washburn

After the United States defeated Little Turtle, Tecumseh, and other Indians of the Ohio Valley, the so-called Old Northwest frontier shifted still farther westward into what are now Illinois, Iowa, Missouri, and Wisconsin. It was in this region that the Sauk, Fox, Kickapoo, Winnebago, and others, led by the capable Black Hawk, made their last stand against the U.S. Army. The tactics the whites used in this war, including the massacre of people (including women and children) carrying white flags, set a precedent for future anti-Indian brutality. Historians Robert M. Utley and Wilcomb E. Washburn, noted authorities on Indian culture, here summarize Black Hawk's valiant but fruitless resistance.

While the government was trying to cope with the Seminoles,[1] settlers far to the north in the Illinois country had been shaken by a brief forlorn Indian revolt in which a warrior named Black Hawk took a last gamble against steep odds. Black Hawk, a chief of the Sauk and Fox Indians—two related tribes that had early joined together—was born in 1767 in a Sauk village on the site of present-day Rock Island, Illinois. He fought his first battle at fifteen, and by the time he reached his thirties he was ably directing armies of more than five hundred Sauk and Foxes against tribal enemies.

In 1804 the United States summoned some Sauk and Fox chieftains to St. Louis, and, after entertaining them lavishly in the grog shops, got them to sign a treaty by which, in re-

1. Creeks, and other southern tribes

Excerpted from Robert M. Utley and Wilcomb E. Washburn, *Indian Wars* (Boston: Houghton Mifflin, 1977). Reprinted by permission of *American Heritage* magazine, a division of Forbes, Inc. © Forbes, Inc.

turn for the usual pittance, they ceded fifty million acres of land. Although Black Hawk's village was included in the cession, the chief was not alarmed at that time because he and his fellows thought the whites merely wanted to use the land for hunting. He subsequently signed a document reaffirming the 1804 treaty, but, he wrote, he "touched the goose quill to the treaty—not knowing . . . that, by that act, I consented to give away my village. Had that been explained to me, I should have opposed it."

Soon white settlers began to move into the territory. Black Hawk became bitter, and his anger and determination grew when he met Tecumseh[2] and heard the great chieftain's compelling message. He fought alongside Tecumseh in the War of 1812 and was with him during his final hours.

In the years following the war, Black Hawk watched the settlers pouring into Illinois. Every year, returning from their winter hunting, the Sauk and Foxes found their lodges burned, their cornfields fenced in, their cemeteries plowed up. Again and again Black Hawk protested to the Indian agents at Rock Island, only to be told that he should move across the Mississippi.

At last, early in 1829, the chieftain returned from a poor hunt to find a white family settled in his own lodge. He got an interpreter and had him tell the squatters "not to settle on our lands—nor trouble our lodges or fences—that there was plenty of land in the country for them to settle upon—and they must leave our village, as we were coming back to it in the spring."

The family ignored the demand, more whites came to settle in the village, and in the summer the General Land Office announced that the area would be put up for public sale in October. For two tense summers Black Hawk returned to stay on his usurped lands. Finally, in April of 1832, the chief, who had spent the winter on the far side of the Mississippi, crossed the river with a band of a thousand men, women, and children, and headed toward his town. The frightened settlers appealed to the Illinois governor, John Reynolds,

2. Shawnee chief who tried to unify many tribes against white encroachment

who, seeing an opportunity to increase his political popular-
ity, called for volunteers to "repel the invasion."

Sixteen hundred men turned out in June and joined regular troops under General Edmund P. Gaines. Gaines, the
commander of the Western Department of the Army, had
fought well against the Creeks and Seminoles with Jackson,
but his volunteers were a poor lot. In mid-May two hundred
seventy-five of them under Major Isaiah Stillman overtook
Black Hawk when the chief was away from his main camp
and had only forty warriors with him. The odds were too
great; Black Hawk sadly sent out a delegation to discuss
terms of surrender. As the Indians approached the camp
under a flag of truce, Stillman's half-drunk militia fired on
them. Black Hawk decided that, if he had to die. he would
die fighting. Marshaling his tiny force, he led what he was
sure was a suicidal attack against the volunteers. As he ran
shouting toward certain death, however, the volunteers
broke and ran. The Indians gave chase for a while, but the
soldiers kept right on going until they reached their main
camp twenty-five miles away. They staggered in all night,
babbling confused accounts of the action, which soon came
to he called Stillman's Run.

Astonished and encouraged by this example of the fighting abilities of the army, Black Hawk went on to lead his
people through the countryside burning farmsteads and taking scalps. The Illinois settlers responded with total hysteria.
A Galena newspaper called for a "war of extermination until
there shall be no Indian (*with his scalp on*) left in . . . Illinois,"
and throughout the states volunteer companies turned out to
hunt down the Indians. One such company, the 1st Regiment of the Brigade of Mounted Volunteers, served under
the amiable command of a New Salem boy named Abraham
Lincoln. During his campaigning, Lincoln said, he never
saw "any live, fighting Indians," though he had "a good
many bloody struggles with the musquitoes." He did, however, witness the scene of a massacre, and the sight stayed
with him for the rest of his life. Years later, in one of his very
few autobiographical reminiscences, he spoke of coming
upon five of Stillman's men, with "the red light of the morn-

ing sun . . . streaming upon them as they lay heads toward us on the ground. And every man had a round, red spot on the top of his head, about as big as a dollar where the redskins had taken his scalp. It was frightful, but it was grotesque; and

Black Hawk Denounces His Captors

After the whites defeated Black Hawk and imprisoned him, he composed a sharp and defiant statement, excerpted here, bitterly accusing them of lying and cheating his people.

An Indian who is as bad as the white men could not live in our nation; he would be put to death, and eaten up by the wolves. The white men are bad schoolmasters; they carry false looks, and deal in false actions; they smile in the face of the poor Indian to cheat him; they shake them by the hand to gain their confidence, to make them drunk, to deceive them, and ruin our wives. We told them to let us alone, but they followed on and beset our paths, and they coiled themselves among us like the snake. They poisoned us by their touch. We were not safe. We lived in danger. We were becoming like them, hypocrites and liars, adulterers, lazy drones, all talkers, and no workers.

We looked up to the Great Spirit. We went to our great father [President Andrew Jackson]. We were encouraged. His great council gave us fair words and big promises, but we got no satisfaction. Things were growing worse. There were no deer in the forest. The opossum and beaver were fled, the springs were drying up, and our squaws and papooses without victuals to keep them from starving; we called a great council and built a large fire. The spirit of our fathers arose and spoke to us to avenge our wrongs or die. . . . We set up the war whoop, and dug up the tomahawk; our knives were ready, and the heart of Black Hawk swelled high in his bosom when he led his warriors to battle. He is satisfied. He will go to the world of spirits contented. He has done his duty. His father will meet him there, and commend him.

Quoted in Annette Rosenstiel, *Red and White: Indian Views of the White Man, 1492–1982.* New York: Universe Books, 1983, pp. 118–20.

the red sunlight seemed to paint everything all over. I remember that one man had on buckskin breeches."

With 150,000 settlers living in Illinois, Black Hawk never had a chance. He did as much damage as he could, but finally, with troops moving toward him on every side, he found himself with half his warriors gone and his back to the Mississippi. Before he could ford the river, the steamboat *Warrior* hove into sight with a detachment of soldiers and a six-pounder[3] aboard. Black Hawk raised a white flag, but the jittery troops responded by opening fire. The Indians sought cover and fired on the ship until she retreated down the river to refuel. Then, early on the morning of August 3, 1,300 volunteers and regulars came storming up to the riverbank. The Indians tried to surrender, but the troops, inflamed by weeks of panic, set upon them clubbing, stabbing, and shooting. The massacre went on for eight hours. When the *Warrior* resumed to add her six-pounder to the carnage, one observer saw the Mississippi "perceptibly tinged with the blood of the Indians who were shot in its margin and in the stream." The soldiers took only thirty-nine prisoners. Two hundred Sauk and Foxes somehow managed to thrash their way across the river only to be scalped or taken prisoner by hostile Sioux, who awaited them on the other side.

Black Hawk managed to survive the slaughter and escaped north to Wisconsin, where he fell in with some Winnebagos who turned him over to the authorities for a reward of a hundred dollars and twenty horses. The chief stayed in jail for a year, and then the government decided to send him on a tour around the country so that the curious could have a chance to get a look at him. He was burned in effigy in Detroit, but by the time he reached the eastern cities, which had not felt the strength of the Indian raids for years, he had become something of a celebrity. Cowed, amiable, his fighting days behind him, he smiled and nodded to the guests at hotel banquets, and they applauded him, a harmless relic of a gaudy past.

3. a kind of cannon

Custer and the Conquest of the Sioux

Royal B. Hassrick

Following the pattern established in the Indian wars in the Ohio Valley, Southeast, and southern Great Lakes region, the Plains Indians found themselves besieged by the on-rush of white settlers and soldiers. The Kiowa, Comanche, Cheyenne, Arapaho, and perhaps the most formidable of all, the Sioux, fought back by raiding white settlements and wagon trains. As Royal B. Hassrick, former curator of the Southern Plains Indians Museum, colorfully tells it here, the culmination of the war for the Great Plains was the Indian victory over George Armstrong Custer at the Little Bighorn in 1876. Unwisely refusing to wait for reinforcements under Generals Crook and Terry, Custer ordered an attack on vastly larger Indian forces and paid the price.

The Plains Indians waged incessant warfare among themselves, and, with the encroachment of the white man, another enemy was added. Valiantly they fought to defend the lands. Kiowa and Comanche raided Texas settlements, continually pillaged caravans of freight and cargo along the Santa Fe Trail, and even waged a pitched battle against the whites at the Adobe Walls. The Sioux and Cheyenne long made travel on the Oregon and Bozeman trails hazardous. Angered at the construction of military forts on their lands, at the railroads cutting the buffalo ranges, the influx of miners scratching for gold in their sacred Black Hills, the Sioux retaliated. Sometimes with assaults on the wagon trains, other times with attacks on the United States Cavalry as-

Excerpted from Royal B. Hassrick, *The Colorful Story of North American Indians* (London: Octopus Books, 1974). Copyright ©1974 by Octopus Books Ltd. Reprinted with permission of the publisher.

signed to protect the trails, the Sioux, under the leadership of Red Cloud, waged war. Outraged, too, at the duplicity of the Washington commissioners who broke treaties before the ink was dry, at the unscrupulous traders rich with graft from short-changing on rations and rotgut whiskey, the Indians' attitude was anything but friendly. The United States, in its self-seeking omnipotence, not only forced treaties upon these Indians, but systematically killed off the buffalo. With the basis of their existence destroyed, the Indians were quite simply starved into submission.

Reno Attacks the Indian Camp

Some Sioux leaders, like Sitting Bull and Crazy Horse, no longer able to endure seeing their people suffer the confinement and shoddy rations of the reservations, defied the government authorities and left. Now they could hunt in freedom. Early in the summer of 1876 a large encampment of Sioux, as well as some Cheyenne and Arapaho, ten to twelve thousand strong, had set their tepees along the west bank of Little Big Horn River in Montana. Sitting Bull, the highly respected headman and powerful shaman, reported having seen in a vision "many soldiers falling into camp." And within a very few days his prophecy came true.

In the early afternoon of 25 June, the Sioux in the Hunkpapa [a branch of the Sioux] village at the north end of the great camp suddenly found themselves being attacked by a cavalry charge of some 140 "bluecoats." The Sioux were quick to respond. Warriors by the hundreds grabbed their weapons, donned their war bonnets and mounted their war ponies to repulse the invaders. And they were marvelously successful. Major Reno, whom the Indians did not know, and his troops were soundly beaten, the major leading a gallant retreat across the river and up the cliffs to a craterlike position which he hoped to defend. The much maligned Reno really had little choice. He was completely outnumbered and the promised support from his commander, the willful and arrogant General George Armstrong Custer, failed to materialize.

No sooner had the Sioux spoiled Reno's plan—and he really didn't have much of a plan, his orders from Custer being simply, "Charge after them, you'll be supported by the whole outfit"—than the Sioux at the north end of the encampment saw troops. About three miles or more from the point of Reno's initial attack, the Indians observed cavalrymen riding along the ridge to the east. At first, a group of five or six valiant Sioux crossed the river hoping to stall the bluecoats' approach, hoping to protect the great camp, the women and children. They were being attacked by the dreaded *wasichu*, the child frightener, the "one who demands," the evil paleface quite properly nicknamed "Bossy."

Within minutes, not tens, not hundreds, but thousands of Indians came to the defense of the brave five or six defenders. More and more soldiers appeared along the ridge—215 of them, it is guessed—as Crazy Horse, Gall and others surged up the hill to surround the scourges. And that is precisely what General Custer was. Authorized to help wipe out the Sioux recalcitrants [defiant ones], he undertook his job

Reno's Retreat

Billy Jackson, a nineteen-year-old Indian scout in Custer's command, later wrote a detailed account of the Little Bighorn campaign. In this exciting excerpt, Jackson and some companions find themselves cut off from Major Reno's unit as it retreats before hundreds of angry Indians.

I saw Major Reno, hatless, a handkerchief tied around his head, getting up on his plunging horse. Waving his six-shooter, he shouted something that I couldn't hear, and led swiftly off, up out of the depression that we were in. We all swarmed after him, and headed back up the way that we had come, our intention being to recross the river and get up onto the bluffs, where we could make a stand. By this time hundreds more of the enemy had come up from the camp, and all together they swarmed in on us and a hand-to-hand fight with them began.

I saw numbers of our men dropping from their horses, saw horses falling, heard their awful neighs of fright and pain. Close ahead of me, Bloody Knife, and then Charlie Reynolds, went down, right there met the fate that they had foretold.

with glee. He also took matters into his own hands, foiling the planned pincer movement of General Terry's troops coming from the North and General Crook's advance from the South. Crook's forces, however, had been absolutely beaten by a Sioux force just eight days before at the Battle of the Rosebud. Crook returned to the safety of Goose Creek like a whipped dog with its tail between its legs. Crook never did show up.

Custer, in splitting his command, brilliantly failed in his promise to reinforce Reno. And poor Reno spent the rest of his life feebly defending himself as the scapegoat for Custer's impetuousness.

The Sioux, Cheyenne and Arapaho, outnumbering Custer's troops by as much as twenty to one, were quick to press their advantage. Black Medicine, or Coffee, a nephew of Crazy Horse, having been wounded in the knee in the Battle of the Rosebud, rode up to observe the fight. "It wasn't much to see.

A big heavy-set Indian brushed up against me, tried to pull me out of the saddle, and I shot him. Then, right in front, a soldier's horse was shot from under him, and as I came up, he grasped my right stirrup and ran beside me. I had to check my horse so that he could keep up, and so began to lag behind. Numbers of Indians were passing on both sides of us, eager to get at the main body of the retreat. At last one of the passing Indians made a close shot at the soldier and killed him, and, as I gave my horse loose rein, Frank Girard came up on my left, and we rode on side by side. Ahead, there was now a solid body of Indians between us and the retreating, hard-pressed soldiers, and Girard shouted to me: "We can't go through them! Let's turn back!"

Indians were still coming on from the direction of their camp, and, as we wheeled off to the left, and then went quartering back toward the timber, several of them shot at us, but we finally got into thick, high brush, dismounted and tied our horses.

Quoted in Jerome A. Greene, ed., *Battles and Skirmishes of the Great Sioux War, 1876–1877: A Military View*. Norman: University of Oklahoma Press, 1993, p. 49.

Too much smoke and dust. It all ended in about the time it takes a man to smoke a pipe." When it was over, when the last man of Custer's troops had been killed, the Sioux harassed Reno's stronghold and they would have destroyed him save for Sitting Bull's forebearing "There has been enough of killing."

Only a Symbolic Victory

The Indians scalped most of Custer's soldiers, stripping them of their uniforms, the women mutilating their bodies to prevent their spirits from haunting the world. Custer, also nicknamed "Long Hair" by the Indians, had had a haircut in accordance with army regulations just before the campaign. His body was found stripped but unmolested, and his scalp was not taken. To the Sioux, the scalp of a suicide was useless, for the spirit of those who committed self-destruction hung forever in limbo, like those of murderers and hermaphrodites [persons born with both male and female reproductive organs]. Custer's body was found with a bullet hole in the chest and one in the temple.

It was a magnificent and symbolic victory for the Indians, but it was short-lived. In less than a year Crazy Horse and his 1100 followers surrendered. Sitting Bull escaped to Canada, but gave himself up in 1881. The power of the Sioux was crushed.

The Tragic Flight of the Nez Percé

J. Jay Myers

In the late 1870s, at the same time that the Plains Indians were making their futile stands against the U.S. Army, the tribes farther west, near the Pacific coast, also faced the bitter choice of relocation or extinction. In 1855, Congress had created the Washington Territory (comprising what are now the states of Washington and Oregon); and in the next two decades white settlers and miners had steadily displaced the region's indigenous Indians. The most celebrated case of native resistance to this white encroachment was that of the Nez Percé, led by Chief Joseph, in 1877. The following riveting account of the tribe's heroic but tragic failed attempt to reach Canada and freedom is from scholar J. Jay Myers's book, *Red Chiefs and White Challengers: Confrontations in American Indian History*.

It was in the year 1900. Chief Joseph was still a prisoner, twenty-three years after he had surrendered and after he had been promised freedom. A "benevolent" government had given him permission to visit his homeland. He went to the grave of his father, and certainly Old Joseph's words came to him again as they had so many times.

> My son, this old body is returning to my mother, earth, and my spirit is going soon, very soon, to see the Great Spirit Chief. . . . When I am gone, think of your country. You are the chief of these people. They look to you to guide them. Always remember your father never sold his country. You must stop your ears whenever you are asked to sign a treaty selling your home. A few years more and the white man will

be all around you. They have their eyes on this land. My son, never forget my dying words: This country holds your father's body. Never sell the bones of your father and mother.

Chief Joseph wept silently. He had never sold the land. He had fought; fought to save the land for his people and fought to keep peace. He had been a man of peace, except for a brief period of two months when the white soldiers came shooting. Then he had no choice, but even then he had tried to prevent the flowing of blood, though it meant leaving the land of his father's grave. . . .

Joseph's people had been in that beautiful country beyond human recall. Called Nez Percés by the French and Chopunnish by Lewis and Clark, their own name was Nimipu, signifying *The People*. They were a very capable people and they were well aware of it. They hunted and they fished, but long before Joseph's era they had become raisers of cattle and horses. Through selective breeding they had developed the Appaloosa horse, which was greatly in demand by all who knew about them. The Appaloosa was distinctive in appearance; a paint with small splashes of color on its hindquarters, a handsome animal. It was mostly desired, however, because it was strong, surefooted in rocky country, seemingly tireless, and well-mannered, even gentle. It was a superb horse for working cattle. The Nez Percés raised enough to sell, at good prices, to whites traveling on the Oregon Trail and later to whites who needed a horse unsurpassed at working cattle in rocky terrain. . . .

A Treaty Forced on Them

Much of the trouble for Old Joseph and his son began with the discovery of gold on the Nez Percé reservation in 1860. Many whites began coming into Nez Percé land and nothing was done about it. By 1861 the trespassing whites—mostly miners—had even established a town called Lewisburg right in the middle of the reservation. There were sixteen hundred inhabitants. Old Joseph and his people had always been friendly with whites, right from their first meeting with Lewis and Clark. Whites had always been able to travel unmolested through Nez Percé country; they could even obtain help when needed. . . . The Nez Percés stood for peace, for peaceful settlement of the broken pledge. They had put up with the government's nonpayment of the purchase price of the Indian land it had "bought." They had put up with the nonfulfillment of the promises to supply schools, teachers, agents, sawmills, gristmills, shops, and mechanics.

But in 1863, the government had decided not to remove the whites from Indian land; instead, the Nez Percés were to be removed. They were to be "given" a piece of land near Lapwai (in Idaho) which was one-eighth of their territory. . . . Old Joseph and the other chiefs living in the southern, or lower, part of Nez Percé country flatly refused even to negotiate. They had given up enough to white greed. The Nez Percés in the north allowed themselves to be swindled, and signed the treaty. Most of those people were Christians and one of their most influential chiefs, Chief Lawyer, who may have been bribed, helped maneuver the treaty.

Old Joseph's band and the other Lower Nez Percés continued to live as though there had been no treaty of 1863. They had not signed it and could not see how it could possibly apply to them. They went about their usual business of raising horses and cattle, they continued to hunt and fish, and they remained on a friendly basis with the whites, selling livestock and buying goods. . . .

Shortly after Old Joseph died [in 1870] a government commission came to talk to the Lower, or nontreaty, Nez Percé chiefs about adjustments to the treaty of 1863. They suggested that perhaps the Nez Percés might be allowed to use the Wallowa Valley if the chiefs would sign the treaty. . . . Chief Joseph and the other chiefs refused to talk about adjustments to the treaty of 1863. They had not signed it. It was of no consequence to them. In 1873, President Ulysses Grant re-ceded the Wallowa area to the Nez Percés. However, the white settlers protested loudly and to the right people, so the re-cession was revoked in 1875, and the land was again officially placed back in the public domain. This meant that Indians could not be on it because they were not part of the public.

Joseph told another commission that his people wanted

only enough land upon which they could graze their horses and cattle. The Wallowa Valley was their winter pasturage. They had to have it and they did not want anything else from the government—no annuities, no agency handouts. . . . Some whites understood, of course, and accepted the Nez Percés as friendly, prosperous neighbors. Some of the whites even knew the land really belonged to the Indians.

The Whites Deliver an Ultimatum

Friction began to develop, however. There were some whites without any scruples at all and they found that somehow the law did not apply whenever it was white versus Indian. Joseph said to a commissioner: "They stole a great many horses from us and we could not get them back because we were Indians. They drove off a great many of our cattle . . . branded our young cattle so they could claim them. We had no friends who would plead our cause."

Between 1860 and 1877, twenty-eight Nez Percés were murdered by whites and not one of the murderers was ever even brought to trial. During the same period not one white was killed by a Nez Percé; still Joseph worked to keep the peace, but his young men were outraged by the white's disregard for the Indians' human and civil rights. It was becoming almost impossible to keep the young men from seeking the time-honored revenge for murder of a relative or friend. But Chief Joseph kept hoping for a change of heart on the part of the white man. He was certain that if one white were killed in retaliation, the whole tribe would be punished. It was a thing whites often did. If one Indian broke the law they would attack the whole tribe—guilt by association.

It didn't even help when Major H. Clay Wood, the assistant adjutant general, was assigned in 1875 to investigate the treaty situation with the Lower Nez Percé bands. He reported that the treaty did not apply to them—they had never signed it and the government had violated the terms anyway. It was "null and void" regarding their occupancy of the Wallowa area. Nevertheless, General Oliver O. Howard was instructed in early 1877 to tell the nontreaty tribes that they must move from their homeland and go to the small tract at

Lapwai Reservation. The treaty was valid and they must abide by it; after all, it had been signed by some Nez Percé chiefs. Chief Joseph replied with clear logic:

> If we ever owned the land we own it still, for we never sold it. In the treaty councils the commissions have claimed that our country had been sold to the government. Suppose a white man should come to me and say, "Joseph, I like your horses, and I want to buy them." I say to him, "No, my horses suit me, I will not sell them." Then he goes to my neighbor, and says to him, "Joseph has some good horses. I want to buy them but he refuses to sell." My neighbor answers, "Pay me the money, and I will sell you Joseph's horses." The white man returns to me, and says, "Joseph, I have bought your horses and you must let me have them." If we sold our lands to the government, this is the way they were bought.

General Howard may or may not have been able to see Joseph's irrefutable argument, but he had his orders and he gave the Lower Nez Percé chiefs an ultimatum. They must be on the move by April 1. The tribes were in a state of indecision. April 1 arrived and the chiefs asked Howard for another council. He granted it, but he could not change his orders. . . . He had no choice but to force the Nez Percé to move to Lapwai Reservation—no bargaining. . . .

Revenge Raids

Chief Joseph could no longer insist the treaty did not apply and go on living as if it didn't. He and the other chiefs had been told to obey the provisions or be killed. Most of the young men wanted to fight. . . . Still Chief Joseph counseled peace, at tremendous cost to himself and to what he believed. The government was wrong, unquestionably. To accede to the outrageous demand was in reality selling "the bones of his father and mother." He had said: "The earth and myself are of one mind. . . . I never said the land was mine to do with as I chose. The one who has a right to dispose of it is the one who created it. I claim a right to live on my land and accord you the privilege to live on yours.". . .

But after great torment Chiefs Joseph, White Bird, and Looking Glass decided they must move to Lapwai. Chief Joseph stated in his memoirs: "I said in my heart that rather than have war I would give up my country. I would give up my father's grave. I would give up everything rather than have the blood of white men upon the hands of my people."

The man of peace set his people to their impossible task of being on the move to Lapwai by June 15. They worked long cruel hours trying to meet the deadline. They lost several hundred head of stock forcing them to swim the cold mountain streams made virtually uncrossable by the melting mountain snow. One herd of cattle could not be taken across a river and the Nez Percés left a small group of warriors to guard it until the waters receded. Some whites attacked the guard and ran off the herd. Joseph managed to prevent war even over that gross injustice.

On June 13, however, a chain of events moved Joseph and his people irrevocably into war. A young warrior had been brooding for two years about the unavenged murder of his father by a drunken white man. The night of June 12 an old man who wanted war taunted him unmercifully about it. The next day the young man found the murderer and killed him. Two other young impatient men accompanied him and killed some white men who had tied them and flogged them without mercy. They rode back to camp and in a frenzy of vengeance persuaded seventeen other young warriors to join them in retaliation for deaths, insults, and robberies. Chief Joseph was not in camp. The young men galloped off, and when they returned they had killed eighteen unfriendly whites.

When Joseph returned to camp the people were panic-stricken. He told them that General Howard would not hold them all responsible for what a few had done, but they knew the white man's guilt-by-association record, and those for war kept stirring up those who were undecided. Finally most of the people decided to go to White Bird Canyon, where they could defend themselves from the white man's retribution that was sure to come. Chief Joseph did not go with them. His wife had given birth to a child and he stayed at the campsite until she could be safely moved. . . .

War Erupts

There was really no chance that the blood already shed would not lead to the shedding of more. When General Howard received the news about the eighteen white deaths, he dispatched two companies of cavalry under Captain David Perry and Captain Joel Trimble to round up the Indians and bring them in for punishment. Chief Joseph had rejoined his people and was still counseling peace. There were ninety-four troopers approaching White Bird Canyon, and Joseph had about sixty men—not all warriors—and perhaps one hundred and twenty women and children. Joseph sent out six men carrying a white flag to see what the soldiers wanted. Unfortunately, there was a volunteer with the soldiers, named Ad Chapman, who had no use for talking to Indians. He raised his rifle and shot at the peace commission. They returned the fire, and the war was on.

The troopers charged into the canyon, right at the lodges they could see before them. The Nez Percés, however, had placed warriors on each side of the canyon. As the soldiers galloped in shooting they were caught in a devastating crossfire. Most of these Nez Percés had never fired a gun at a man, but they were good hunters and this situation was much like hunting. Thirty-four cavalrymen died in that battle. . . .

After the affair at White Bird Canyon the Indians crossed the Salmon River and took positions to thwart General Howard's troops whom they knew would soon be on their trail. Howard was discouraged when he arrived at the Salmon and wrote: "No general could have chosen a safer position or one more likely to puzzle and obstruct a foe." He did manage to cross the river, and he plunged into the forest after the retreating Indians only to find out in a few days that they were no longer retreating. They had swung around and were now at his rear—cutting off his supplies. If the Indians had cared to do so, they could have ravaged and looted the white settlements while Howard's troops fought their way out of the heavy forest. They did not, however, at any time during the war, nor did they ever scalp or otherwise mutilate dead soldiers. . . .

After the Salmon River fiasco Howard added some more

troops to his army and set off to find the Nez Percés, who had all their noncombatants and two thousand horses to move along. The Indians chose a spot on the Clearwater River for another stand. Howard sent in a cavalry charge and blasted the Nez Percés with howitzers and Gatling guns, but the Indians had "dug in" and were shooting from behind mounds of earth and well-placed logs. The battle lasted a day and a half. The big guns took a toll among the warriors and the women and children, and Howard had thirteen soldiers killed and twenty-seven wounded. But he was suddenly left on the field with no one to fight. The noncombatants, under Joseph, had struck camp and, driving their huge horse herd, had been on the trail for hours before the warriors melted back into the forests and left Howard with nothing to show for the dead and wounded the battle had cost him.

Battle at Big Hole River

After the fight at Clearwater, Joseph called a council to find the will of his people about the next step. Should they stay and fight, should they try to reach Canada, or should they surrender and hope for the best? . . .

The people voted to flee to Canada. They hoped the Crows might help them, and perhaps Sitting Bull [the renowned Sioux chief who had helped defeat Custer] would come down from his self-imposed exile for one more shot at the United States army. They believed they could make it to the border without any help if it was necessary. Joseph went with his people, with the warriors, the women, babies in mothers' arms, the old and feeble, the sick—and the two thousand horses. The horses, the men said, would make it possible to succeed. The soldiers would be riding the same horses mile after mile, day after day, but the Nez Percés would have fresh remounts.

Right into the Bitterroot Mountains they went, with General Howard pressing hard. Up and over the rocky, perilous Lolo Pass. The going was slow for the Indian cavalcade but it was even slower for the big cavalry horses and the white soldiers with all their paraphernalia of war. The Indians began to open up distance between them and the troops.

Howard realized it and for the first time in the campaign used a medium of communication the Indians neither had nor knew. Howard used the telegraph. He directed that troops be sent to a strategic place where the Indians would be dropping down into the Bitterroot Valley in Montana. A Captain Charles C. Rawn hurried there with the few soldiers he had available to him, along with some civilian volunteers. They hastily threw up a fort, hoping to stop the Indians until Howard could catch up.

The war leaders were exceedingly clever. They made a sizable commotion in front of the fort which held the troopers' attention while the rest of the caravan went around the fort by using a narrow mountain trail thought to be impassable for a large group. The civilians in the area dubbed Rawn's fort "Fort Fizzle.". . .

When the Nez Percés had crossed the valley east to the Big Hole River they stopped to rest. General Howard was still in the mountains. But again he used the telegraph. This time it was a message to Colonel John Gibbon at Fort Shawl. Gibbon left immediately with two hundred troops, traveling southwest as fast as he could.

At dawn on August 9, Gibbon slipped down from a wooded height. A boy watering horses saw them and shrieked a warning. The troopers rushed in among the lodges and shot indiscriminately at men, women, and children as they rushed out of their tepees. The valiant flight to freedom should have ended there. But Too-hul-hul-sote, White Bird, Ollokot, and Looking Glass organized the warriors at the outer edge of the camp and they began pouring a deadly fire into the soldiers. Gibbon ordered the tepees burned, but a heavy dew made them too damp for that and Gibbon found his situation to be untenable. He had many wounded and dead soldiers and he had a serious leg wound. He withdrew up the hill from which he had attacked. . . . For the troops, it was twenty-nine dead and forty wounded. For the Nez Percés there may have been fifty women and children dead—including two of Joseph's wives. There were warriors too who would not fight again, and the indispensable Looking Glass had been killed. . . .

Freedom in Sight

The Nez Percés now had to travel fast, no matter the suffering of the many wounded, because General Howard was pushing hard and rapidly closing up on them. They headed south for Targhee Pass, hoping to get over the Continental Divide, but Howard was coming so fast that he had to be slowed down or stopped, whatever the risk. A bold plan was conceived. Forty Indian scouts of Howard's were known to be in the path of the Nez Percés in the vicinity of Targhee Pass. The plan was to send forty Nez Percés into Howard's camp at night as though they were the scouts returning to report. The forty daring Nez Percés rode audaciously in columns of four right into the camp, past the pickets, and began stampeding horses and the mules for the pack train. They shot troopers as they stumbled out of their tents. They especially made certain the pack mules were scattered far and wide. Then they returned to their own camp, knowing Howard was hamstrung.

General Howard was out of the action until he could obtain more pack mules, and he had many wounded. Gibbon, of course, was out of contention, too. The Nez Percés hurried on, through Targhee Pass and into Yellowstone Park. There were a few tourists there and the Nez Percés had to take them captive, but allowed them to escape a few days later, unharmed. But the traveling was excruciatingly slow with the wounded and the now rapidly tiring horses.

Out of Yellowstone the Nez Percés headed north toward freedom. But the telegraph wires had been singing again and this time it was Colonel Samuel Sturgis with six companies of the Seventh Cavalry—Custer's old outfit still looking for revenge. At Clark's Fork Canyon he placed himself squarely across the Indians' path, but they adroitly avoided a fight by flanking him as they forced their way through the tortuous windings of a rocky dry river bed. Sturgis was completely fooled, but he had fresh troops and horses and was soon on their trail. . . .

Joseph's people fled blindly on, in unfamiliar territory, heading north. . . . As desperate as the situation was, the Indians began to feel real hope for the first time. They had taken some much needed supplies from a military depot and they had finally crossed the Missouri River. They still had all the problems of the suffering wounded, the exhausted old and feeble, and the skeletonlike horses, but they were approaching the boundary. They had Howard outdistanced. They had traveled about eighteen hundred tortured miles and they had fought off a combined total of about three thousand troops.

When they reached the north slope of Bear Paw Mountain they could see the promised land. At the bottom of the mountain they were thirty miles from the border—one day's march and Howard was two days behind. Surely they could rest one day—one day's respite for the hollow-eyed, emaciated people, one day for the dying horses before the last day's push. They had beaten all adversaries and all adversity. Freedom would soon be theirs. . . .

The Final Battle

Again, however, General Howard had used the telegraph. Colonel Nelson Miles was traveling light and fast from Fort Keough with 375 men and some cannon. He had been very lucky. He had figured the Nez Percés to be three or four days south of the Missouri. He had met two white trappers who told him they had seen the Indians cross the river two days before. Miles crossed the river and pushed even faster. On September 30 Crow scouts found the Nez Percé trail, and on October 3 Miles surprised the Indian one-day-of-rest camp. His men and his horses were fresh. He had plenty of ammunition and rations. He attacked from three sides.

These Indians did not panic as Indians were expected to. They answered the attack with deadly fire, knocking officers and men out of their saddles. The Nez Percé camp was in a ravine but there were sharpshooters on the bluffs around it. One hundred and fifty troopers started up to capture one well-placed group of riflemen and fifty-three died or were wounded—only to find when they had achieved the height that the Indians had evacuated. But the lodges were surrounded and the Indian fighters found they had been separated into two groups. Chief Joseph put his small daughter on a horse and she escaped—eventually getting to Sitting Bull's camp. Joseph, the nonwarrior, took a rifle and joined the defense.

Miles ordered a cavalry charge but the Indians emptied so many saddles the charge was turned back. Other charges were ordered, and stopped. Then Joseph was told that Ollokot had been killed. The death of his brother, the much loved warrior of the family, seemed suddenly to fill Joseph with the futility of it all.

When night fell Miles laid siege to the camp. He had little to show for all his casualties. In the morning he no longer sent soldiers charging at the death-dealing warriors but used his cannon in an effort to destroy the lives and lodges of the beleaguered Nez Percés. After several hours of the lethal barrage he sent troopers in to finish the job, but they were again met with withering fire and withdrew. Just before dark General Howard arrived with his staff. His army would be along soon. . . .

Surrender and Relocation

At dawn's light Miles and Howard saw a white flag on a pole in the Indian camp. A messenger brought word that Chief Joseph would come to surrender that day. He didn't come until nearly sunset. An officer described him: "His scalp lock was tied with otter fur. The rest of his hair hung in a thick plait on each side of his head. He wore buckskin leggings and a gray woolen shawl through which there were the marks of four or five bullets received in the last conflict. His head and wrists were also scratched with bullets." He came riding with his head bowed, his hands clasped on the saddle pommel, a rifle across his knees. Five warriors walked by the side of his horse. When he came near Miles and Howard he straightened himself. With head erect he gracefully slid from his saddle, walked to Howard and held out his rifle, butt first—signal of peace. Howard indicated Joseph should give it to Miles, which he did.

With great dignity he addressed the victors:

I am tired of fighting. Our chiefs are killed. Looking Glass is

dead. Too-hul-hul-sote is dead. The old men are all dead. . . .
Oh, it is cold and we have no blankets. The little children are
freezing to death. My people, some of them, have run away
into the hills, and have no blankets, no food. No one knows
where they are—perhaps they are freezing to death. I want
to have time to look for my children, and see how many of
them I can find. Maybe I shall find them all among the dead.
Hear me, my chiefs . . . ; my heart is sick and sad. From
where the sun now stands, I will fight no more, forever!

The long unfair, uneven campaign had ended, as it had to
end, with defeat. Miles promised Joseph that he and his survivors would be taken to Lapwai Reservation, which was
where they were going before the three young men killed the
whites. Miles had superiors, however, who had other ideas.

The Nez Percés who were still alive were placed on flat-
boats and taken down the Missouri all the way to Fort Leavenworth. Later they were put in boxcars and shunted around
on railroads until they were finally put off in Indian Territory (now Oklahoma). There they were handed some seeds
and some old worn-out implements, and told to scratch out
a living for themselves.

These proud mountain people, superb horsemen, horse
breeders and cattle raisers, did not know how to make a living as farmers. They began to die. They died from starvation
and from malaria, for which they had no resistance. Nearly
half of them died in Indian territory. . . .

Joseph and his people continued to wait and pray. And
Nelson Miles worked to make amends. He fought every one
he could fight. He proclaimed that what was done to the
Nez Percés was a violation of surrender terms and of his
honor and the honor of the United States. . . . Not even the
popular and famous Nelson Miles could obtain any redress
of wrongs. Someone finally did take action, though, when it
appeared there might soon be no Nez Percés alive. In 1885,
the order came from Washington to return them to the
Northwest. Most of those who had managed to survive were
taken to Lapwai. . . . "Most," however, did not include Chief
Joseph. He was deemed a troublemaker who should not be

with his people. He was sent to the Colville Reservation in northern Washington. . . .

From 1885, almost until his death, he petitioned to be reunited with his people. He was once allowed to go to Washington to plead his case to President Theodore Roosevelt. The president courteously heard him out, but did nothing. Finally he asked only to be allowed to live out his few remaining years as an individual in the Wallowa Valley he loved so dearly, near his father's grave. Someone in authority did eventually grant permission for his brief visit in 1900. He died of a stroke in 1904 on Colville Reservation in northern Washington.

Today an impressive granite shaft marks Chief Joseph's grave, but it is a long way from his father's bones in Wallowa Valley.

U.S. Subjugation of the Apache and Navajo

Edward H. Spicer

The Navajo, Apache, and other tribes inhabiting the arid lands of the Southwest long had only minimal contact with American traders and settlers, mainly because their ancestral lands were part of Mexico. Beginning in the late 1840s, however, the United States acquired these lands in the treaty settlement ending the Mexican-American War; and the local Indians, like their brethren in the Ohio Valley, the Plains, and the Pacific Northwest, found themselves suddenly wide open to white settlement and exploitation. As former University of Arizona scholar Edward H. Spicer explains here, the experiences of various tribes, both in warfare with the whites and in the subsequent relocation process, were often quite different. The Navajo, for example, were conquered relatively quickly, yet they adjusted to subjugation reasonably well considering the deplorable way they were treated. By contrast, the Apache, among the most effective guerrilla fighters in history, held out against the U.S. Army for many years; and once beaten, they found it difficult to adjust to their new white-controlled world.

New conditions of life came rapidly to the southwestern tribes after 1848. The peace of Guadeloupe Hidalgo between Mexico and the United States meant a new regime for the Pueblos, east and west, the Navajos and Apaches, and the Yuman and Piman speaking peoples of Arizona. Those who were to be most drastically changed by the appearance of new military power were the Athabascan-speaking Navajos and Apaches. . . . Their way of life had altered sharply as a result of the domestic animals introduced by the Spaniards and by the opportunities which faltering Spanish and Mexican control of the region opened up for exploitation of the settled peoples, both Indian and European. This herding and raiding existence dependent on the farming communities of others had become the way of life for the Athabascan-speaking peoples by 1848. Mexican control was weak, and the border had been unstable for nearly seventy years.

New Enemies Appear for the Apache and Navajo

The expectation of the Apaches and Navajos was that they would and should have a freer hand in raiding the Mexican settlements. The Americans had not fought either the Apaches or Navajos. It was therefore inconceivable to the Indians that the Americans could regard their hunting and raiding ranges as United States territory. The Indians had never been conquered by the Mexicans and hence in the Indian view they still held their lands. It came as a shock to find that the Americans regarded their victory over the Mexicans as also a victory over the Indians of the region, especially when parleys indicated at the beginning that the Americans wished to prohibit raiding against the Indians' old enemies—the Mexicans. The first feelers with the American expeditionary leaders left no mistake about the American view. Apaches and Navajos knew from that point on that they had acquired new enemies, not new allies as they had hoped.

There was little actual change until after the Civil War, although several bands of both Navajos and Apaches made contact with Americans before 1860. But rapidly as troops came into the New Mexico territory toward the end of the Civil War, it became clear to the Indians that they were going to have to fight for their hunting ranges and for their independence. The Americans gathered a group of war leaders among the Navajos and executed a treaty at Bear Springs in 1864. They treated with Gila Apaches near the Santa Rita Mines in eastern New Mexico. As in the early days of contact with the Plains tribes it became apparent to Americans that treaties were not going to gain their ends, so long as there was no general authority among the tribes. The Navajos were stimulated to some unaccustomed unity by the building of Fort Defiance and other posts in the heart of their range in northeastern Arizona. There was some banding together of the many groups, not only war leaders and their supporters for offensive raids, but also peace leaders. No extensive unity was achieved, however, and the Navajos quickly found themselves fighting for survival quite separate

---

Calling on the Spirits for Help

Perhaps the most famous and feared Apache leader was Goyathlay (ca.1829–1909), who came to be best known by the name the Mexicans gave him—Geronimo. He fought under the Apache chief Cochise in the 1860s and then himself led a stubborn guerrilla war against the U.S. Army in the 1870s and 1880s. Because of his frequent successes as a warrior, many Indians believed that he possessed mystical powers, as explained here by Norman Bancroft-Hunt, a noted scholar of Indian culture.

The Apache was said to be able to 'travel as invisibly as a ghost [and] appear or disappear as silently as a shadow'. A legendary example of this comes from the Chiricahua, when a band of warriors was surrounded by a vastly superior force of U.S. soldiers. Realizing their situation was desperate, the war leader and shaman, Geronimo, pointed to a distant mountain, telling his men they should slip through the ranks of soldiers guarding their position and rendezvous on the mountain in four days. Using his shamanic power, Geronimo called on the spirits for help and a small sandstorm blew up, stinging the eyes of the soldiers and making it difficult for them to observe the movements of the Apaches. The warriors crawled from their hiding places, each holding on to the heel of the man in front, and in this manner passed between the soldiers, sometimes so closely that it is said they could hear their breathing. Geronimo's amazing feat is still commemorated today in a Fire Dance song of the Chiricahua.

Norman Bancroft-Hunt, *Warriors: Warfare and the Native American Indian.* London: Salamander Books, 1995, p. 127.

from one another in different parts of their large territory. One Navajo named Manuelito emerged as something of a general peace leader, but he achieved no wider unity than any single Sioux leader had been able to muster. The Americans, under the leadership of Kit Carson, organized a systematic scorched earth conquest. Large numbers of the sheep on which the Navajos had become heavily dependent were killed, and bands of Navajos were systematically pursued into the farthest hideouts such as Canyon de Chelly. At the end of 1865 the Navajos were largely without food and began to give in, band by band. Only a few hundred remained hidden, to escape the Americans.

The Navajos' "Long Walk"

The Americans immediately instituted a plan for converting the Navajos into farmers. Instead of leaving them within their range in New Mexico Territory, they forced the Indians to move en masse to Fort Sumner some 250 miles eastward on the edge of the Plains. This forced migration became known to the Navajos as the "Long Walk." They were placed, together with Apaches such as the Mescaleros who had also been rounded up, on a small fenced reservation [at Bosque Redondo]. The American plan called for getting the Navajos to live in adobe houses, to farm, and to develop peaceful community life under the strict supervision of Army officers. The plan differed from that tried with the Plains Indians chiefly in that mutually hostile tribes were placed together and that the new location was at a great distance from their homeland.

The plan did not work. This became apparent within a year, and the Americans decided in 1868 to make a new treaty with the Navajos. This called for return to their old stamping grounds which were guaranteed to the Navajos free of trespass by Whites, the issue of sheep, attendance at schools with one teacher for every 30 Navajo children, and of course agreement by the Navajos to stop raiding and to remain at peace. With conclusion of the treaty the Navajos were faced with returning as best they could to their homeland—the second phase of the "Long Walk."

Adjusting to Life on the Reservation

The incarceration at Fort Sumner had impressed the Navajos with the power of the Americans. It opened a new era in Navajo life. Their new reservation was large and was not yet attractive to Whites. The government began the issue of hundreds of sheep. The Navajos spread out again and began to develop their mixed herding-agricultural economy much as before but without reliance on raiding. The reservation was increased rather than reduced in size during the next thirty years and only a small part was subjected to allotment in the 1890s. Under these circumstances Navajo life blossomed. Their population began to increase. They developed not only the herding of sheep and horses but also blanket weaving which they had adapted from Pueblos and Spaniards.

The stay at Fort Sumner had resulted in some new tribal organization, or at least the dominance of Manuelito and several other peace leaders, so that foundations were laid for more unified political life. By the late 1890s they were one of the more prosperous tribes under the reservation system. They were relatively little interfered with by Indian agents because of the great extent of their territory. They resisted sending their children to school. They were developing a new life which was rooted deeply in their two century adaptation of sheepherding. They were encouraged by the Bureau of Indian Affairs to develop an economy based on what they already knew. At the same time the Catholic Franciscans instituted missions which became an important source of contacts and the learning of some White ways, but only small numbers became Christians. So well adapted were they under the particular non-restrictive reservation situation that no Messiah arose among them. They rejected the Ghost Dance [the new religious movement that during the late 1880s spread from the Indians of the Great Basin—where it began as a peaceful, positive attempt to restore traditional Indian values and ways of life—to the Indians of the plains where its increasing militancy was misinterpreted by U.S. Indian agents and soldiers ultimately leading to the Massacre at Wounded Knee in 1890] partly because its stress on the return of the dead conflicted with Navajo values, but also because they were not in desperate circumstances either with respect to economic conditions or loss of political autonomy.

In contrast, the transition for Apaches was more destructive, and solid foundations for a new peaceful life were not laid. The Apache lands were in the midst of mining and cattle developments in Arizona and New Mexico. The Jicarillas were rounded up quickly and isolated on a small reservation in northern New Mexico. The Chiricahua, the San Carlos, the White Mountain, the Tonto, and Gila Apaches did not experience such easy transition. Silver and gold mines were opened up in various parts of their range, and settlers moved into the relatively desirable valleys of the Arizona area. There were many Apache frontiers, and numerous massacres and conflicts. No one Army campaign was successful in starving them into submission. The Army was, in fact, in their rugged domain no match for the various hard-fighting Apache bands, until a campaign was designed to infiltrate their whole country with forts as bases for constantly active cavalry forces. The Army attempted to concentrate them in five different places, a major one being at San Carlos in central Arizona. For more than fifteen years the Army struggled to force the Apaches to remain on reservations. Able war leaders such as Cochise [and Victoria, Nana, and Geronimo] appeared among them. It was not until 1887 that stability under Army control was finally established. Meanwhile one prophet, Nakai-doklini, arose in the White Mountains of Arizona and was promptly shot by U.S. Cavalry. After 1887 the Apaches were established on five reservations—San Carlos, Fort Apache, and Camp Verde in Arizona and Jicarilla and Mescalero in New Mexico. There had not developed among them any unifying leadership. Their subjugation under Army rule was complete in the 1890s. They settled down to a life of rations, as the Indian agents sought to encourage them to take up farming.

The Ghost Dance and Wounded Knee Massacre

Dee Brown

By 1890, the U.S. conquest of the Native Americans was, for all intents and purposes, complete. In the waning months of that fateful year, in one last collective wail of sadness and desperation, thousands of Indians embraced a new religion, the Ghost Dance, which promised the miraculous destruction of the white civilization and salvation of the red. In this essay, constituting the final section of her widely acclaimed and moving book, *Bury My Heart at Wounded Knee*, renowned scholar of Indian history Dee Brown recounts the coming of the Ghost Dance. Then she tells how, as had happened so often before, lack of understanding and sympathy on the part of whites led to fear, which in turn led to violence. The tragic massacre at Wounded Knee was the last major engagement of the American Indian Wars.

In the Drying Grass Moon (October 9, 1890) . . . a Minneconjou from the Cheyenne River agency came to Standing Rock to visit Sitting Bull. His name was Kicking Bear, and he brought news of the Paiute Messiah, Wovoka, who had founded the religion of the Ghost Dance. Kicking Bear and his brother-in-law, Short Bull, had returned from a long journey beyond the Shining Mountains in search of the Messiah. Hearing of this pilgrimage, Sitting Bull had sent for Kicking Bear in order to learn more about the Ghost Dance.

Kicking Bear told Sitting Bull of how a voice had commanded him to go forth and meet the ghosts of Indians who were to return and inhabit the earth. On the cars of the Iron

Horse [train] he and Short Bull and nine other Sioux had traveled far toward the place where the sun sets, traveled until the railroad stopped. There they were met by two Indians they had never seen before, but who greeted them as brothers and gave them meat and bread. They supplied the pilgrims with horses and they rode for four suns until they came to a camp of Fish Eaters (Paiutes) near Pyramid Lake in Nevada.

The Fish Eaters told the visitors that Christ had returned to earth again. Christ must have sent for them to come there, Kicking Bear said; it was foreordained. To see the Messiah they had to make another journey to the agency at Walker Lake.

For two days Kicking Bear and his friends waited at Walker Lake with hundreds of other Indians speaking in dozens of different tongues. These Indians had come from many reservations to see the Messiah.

Just before sundown on the third day the Christ appeared, and the Indians made a big fire to throw light on him. Kicking Bear had always thought that Christ was a white man like the missionaries, but this man looked like an Indian. After a while he rose and spoke to the waiting crowd. "I have sent for you and am glad to see you," he said. "I am going to talk to you after a while about your relatives who are dead and gone. My children, I want you to listen to all I have to say to you. I will teach you how to dance a dance, and I want you to dance it. Get ready for your dance, and when the dance is over, I will talk to you." Then he commenced to dance, everybody joining in, the Christ singing while they danced. They danced the Dance of the Ghosts until late at night, when the Messiah told them they had danced enough.

Next morning, Kicking Bear and the others went up close to the Messiah to see if he had the scars of crucifixion which the missionaries on the reservations had told them about. There was a scar on his wrist and one on his face, but they could not see his feet, because he was wearing moccasins. Throughout the day he talked to them. In the beginning, he said, God made the earth, and then sent the Christ to earth to teach the people, but white men had treated him badly, leaving scars on his body, and so he had gone back to heaven. Now he had returned to earth as an Indian, and he was to renew everything as it used to be and make it better.

In the next springtime, when the grass was knee high, the earth would be covered with new soil which would bury all the white men, and the new land would be covered with sweet grass and running water and trees. Great herds of buffalo and wild horses would come back. The Indians who danced the Ghost Dance would be taken up in the air and suspended there while a wave of new earth was passing, and then they would be set down among the ghosts of their ancestors on the new earth, where only Indians would live. . . .

The Soldiers Begin to March

Sitting Bull listened to all that Kicking Bear had to relate about the Messiah and the Ghost Dance. He did not believe it was possible for dead men to return and live again, but his people had heard of the Messiah and were fearful he would pass them by and let them disappear when the new resurrection came, unless they joined in the dancing. Sitting Bull had no objections to his people dancing the Ghost Dance, but he had heard that agents at some reservations were bringing soldiers in to stop the ceremonies. He did not want soldiers coming in to frighten and perhaps shoot their guns at his people. Kicking Bear replied that if the Indians wore the sacred garments of the Messiah—Ghost Shirts painted with magic symbols—no harm could come to them. Not even the bullets of the Bluecoats' guns could penetrate a Ghost Shirt.

With some skepticism, Sitting Bull invited Kicking Bear to remain with his band at Standing Rock and teach them the Dance of the Ghosts. This was in the Moon of Falling Leaves, and across the West on almost every Indian reservation the Ghost Dance was spreading like a prairie fire under a high wind. Agitated Indian Bureau inspectors and Army officers from Dakota to Arizona, from Indian Territory to Nevada, were trying to fathom the meaning of it. By early autumn the official word was: Stop the Ghost Dancing.

"A more pernicious system of religion could not have been offered to a people who stood on the threshold of civilization," White Hair [James] McLaughlin said. Although he was a practicing Catholic, McLaughlin, like most other agents, failed to recognize the Ghost Dance as being entirely Christian. Except for a difference in rituals, its tenets were the same as those of any Christian church.

"You must not hurt anybody or do harm to anyone. You must not fight. Do right always," the Messiah commanded. Preaching nonviolence and brotherly love, the doctrine called for no action by the Indians except to dance and sing. The Messiah would bring the resurrection.

But because the Indians were dancing, the agents became alarmed and notified the soldiers, and the soldiers began to march.

The Dance Spreads Across the Plains

A week after Kicking Bear came to Standing Rock to teach Sitting Bull's people the Ghost Dance, White Hair McLaughlin sent a dozen Indian police to remove him from the reservation. Awed by Kicking Bear's aura of holiness, the policemen referred McLaughlin's order to Sitting Bull, but the chief refused to take action. On October 16 McLaughlin sent a larger force of police, and this time Kicking Bear was escorted off the reservation.

The following day McLaughlin notified the Commissioner of Indian Affairs that the real power behind the "pernicious system of religion" at Standing Rock was Sitting Bull. He recommended that the chief be arrested, removed from the reservation, and confined to a military prison. The commissioner conferred with the Secretary of War, and they decided that such action would create more trouble than it would prevent.

By mid-November Ghost Dancing was so prevalent on the Sioux reservations that almost all other activities came to a halt. No pupils appeared at the schoolhouses, the trading stores were empty, no work was done on the little farms. At Pine Ridge the frightened agent telegraphed Washington: "Indians are dancing in the snow and are wild and crazy. . . . We need protection and we need it now. The leaders should be arrested and confined at some military post until the matter is quieted, and this should be done at once."

Short Bull led his band of believers down White River into the Badlands, and in a few days their numbers swelled to more than three thousand. Disregarding the wintry weather, they donned their Ghost Shirts and danced from each dawn far into the nights. Short Bull told the dancers not to fear the soldiers if they came to stop the ceremonies. "Their horses will sink into the earth," he said. "The riders will jump from their horses, but they will sink into the earth also."

At Cheyenne River, Big Foot's band increased to six hundred, mostly widows. When the agent tried to interfere, Big Foot took the dancers off the reservation to a sacred place on Deep Creek.

On November 20 the Indian Bureau in Washington ordered agents in the field to telegraph the names of all "fomenters of disturbances" among the Ghost Dancers. A list was quickly assembled in Washington, and transmitted to Bear Coat [Nelson] Miles's Army headquarters in Chicago. Miles saw Sitting Bull's name among the "fomenters" and immediately assumed that he was to blame for all the disturbances. Miles knew that a forced arrest by soldiers would create trouble; he wanted Sitting Bull removed quietly [but it did not work out as he had desired. The army sent forty-three Indian police to arrest Sitting Bull and when a crowd of Ghost Dancers interfered, shots rang out. Sitting Bull and several of the Indian police were slain.] . . .

A White Flag Is Raised

Had it not been for the sustaining force of the Ghost Dance religion, the Sioux in their grief and anger over the assassination of Sitting Bull might have risen up against the guns of the soldiers. So prevalent was their belief that the white men would soon disappear and that with the next greening of the grass their dead relatives and friends would return, they made no retaliations. By the hundreds, however, the leaderless Hunkpapas fled from Standing Rock, seeking refuge in one of the Ghost Dance camps or with the last of the great chiefs, Red Cloud, at Pine Ridge. In the Moon When the Deer Shed Their Horns (December 17) about a hundred of these fleeing Hunkpapas reached Big Foot's Minneconjou camp near Cherry Creek. That same day the War Department issued orders for the arrest and imprisonment of Big Foot. He was on the list of "fomenters of disturbances."

As soon as Big Foot learned that Sitting Bull had been killed, he started his people toward Pine Ridge, hoping that Red Cloud could protect them from the soldiers. En route, he fell ill of pneumonia, and when hemorrhaging began, he had to travel in a wagon. On December 28, as they neared Porcupine Creek, the Minneconjous sighted four troops of cavalry approaching. Big Foot immediately ordered a white flag run up over his wagon. About two o'clock in the afternoon he raised up from his blankets to greet Major Samuel Whitside, Seventh U.S. Cavalry. Big Foot's blankets were stained with blood from his lungs, and as he talked in a hoarse whisper with Whitside, red drops fell from his nose and froze in the bitter cold.

Whitside told Big Foot that he had orders to take him to a cavalry camp on Wounded Knee Creek. The Minneconjou chief replied that he was going in that direction; he was taking his people to Pine Ridge for safety.

Turning to his half-breed scout, John Shangreau, Major Whitside ordered him to begin disarming Big Foot's band.

"Look here, Major," Shangreau replied, "if you do that, there is liable to be a fight here; and if there is, you will kill all those women and children and the men will get away from you."

Whitside insisted that his orders were to capture Big Foot's Indians and disarm and dismount them.

"We better take them to camp and then take their horses from them and their guns," Shangreau declared.

"All right," Whitside agreed. "You tell Big Foot to move down to camp at Wounded Knee."

The major glanced at the ailing chief, and then gave an order for his Army ambulance to be brought forward. The ambulance would be warmer and would give Big Foot an easier ride than the jolting springless wagon. After the chief was transferred to the ambulance, Whitside formed a column for the march to Wounded Knee Creek. Two troops of cavalry took the lead, the ambulance and wagons following, the Indians herded into a compact group behind them, with the other two cavalry troops and a battery of two Hotchkiss guns bringing up the rear.

Arrival at Wounded Knee

Twilight was falling when the column crawled over the last rise in the land and began descending the slope toward Chankpe Opi Wakpala, the creek called Wounded Knee. The wintry dusk and the tiny crystals of ice dancing in the dying light added a supernatural quality to the somber landscape. Somewhere along this frozen stream the heart of Crazy Horse lay in a secret place, and the Ghost Dancers believed that his disembodied spirit was waiting impatiently for the new earth that would surely come with the first green grass of spring.

At the cavalry tent camp on Wounded Knee Creek, the Indians were halted and carefully counted. There were 120 men and 230 women and children. Because of the gathering darkness, Major Whitside decided to wait until morning before disarming his prisoners. He assigned them a camping area immediately to the south of the military camp, issued them rations, and as there was a shortage of tepee covers, he furnished them several tents. Whitside ordered a stove placed in Big Foot's tent and sent a regimental surgeon to administer to the sick chief. To make certain that none of his prisoners escaped, the major stationed two troops of cavalry as sentinels around the Sioux tepees, and then posted his two Hotchkiss guns on top of a rise overlooking the camp. The barrels of these rifled guns, which could hurl explosive charges for more than two miles, were positioned to rake the length of the Indian lodges.

Later in the darkness of that December night the remainder of the Seventh Regiment marched in from the east and quietly bivouacked north of Major Whitside's troops. Colonel James W. Forsyth, commanding Custer's former regiment, now took charge of operations. He informed Whitside that he had received orders to take Big Foot's band to the Union Pacific Railroad for shipment to a military prison in Omaha. . . .

The Search for Weapons

"The following morning there was a bugle call," said Wasumaza, one of Big Foot's warriors who years afterward was to change his name to Dewey Beard. "Then I saw the soldiers mounting their horses and surrounding us. It was announced that all men should come to the center for a talk and that after the talk they were to move on to Pine Ridge agency. Big Foot was brought out of his tepee and sat in front of his tent and the older men were gathered around him and sitting right near him in the center."

After issuing hardtack for breakfast rations, Colonel Forsyth informed the Indians that they were now to be disarmed. "They called for guns and arms," White Lance said, "so all of us gave the guns and they were stacked up in the center." The soldier chiefs were not satisfied with the number of weapons surrendered, and so they sent details of troopers to search the tepees. "They would go right into the tents and come out with bundles and tear them open," Dog Chief said. "They brought our axes, knives, and tent stakes and piled them near the guns."

Still not satisfied, the soldier chiefs ordered the warriors to remove their blankets and submit to searches for weapons. The Indians' faces showed their anger, but only the medicine man, Yellow Bird, made any overt protest. He danced a few Ghost Dance steps, and chanted one of the holy songs, assuring the warriors that the soldiers' bullets could not penetrate their sacred garments. "The bullets will not go toward you," he chanted in Sioux. "The prairie is large and the bullets will not go toward you."

The troopers found only two rifles, one of them a new Winchester belonging to a young Minneconjou named Black Coyote. Black Coyote raised the Winchester above his head, shouting that he paid much money for the rifle and that it belonged to him. Some years afterward Dewey Beard recalled that Black Coyote was deaf. "If they had left him alone he was going to put his gun down where he should. They grabbed him and spinned him in the east direction. He was still unconcerned even then. He hadn't his gun pointed at anyone. His intention was to put that gun down. They came on and grabbed the gun that he was going to put down. Right after they spun him around there was the report of a gun, was quite loud. I couldn't say that anybody was shot, but following that was a crash.". . .

"They shot us like we were buffalo."

Turning Hawk said that Black Coyote . . . fired his gun and that "immediately the soldiers returned fire and indiscriminate killing followed."

In the first seconds of violence, the firing of carbines was deafening, filling the air with powder smoke. Among the dying who lay sprawled on the frozen ground was Big Foot. Then there was a brief lull in the rattle of arms, with small groups of Indians and soldiers grappling at close quarters, using knives, clubs, and pistols. As few of the Indians had arms, they soon had to flee, and then the big Hotchkiss guns on the hill opened up on them, firing almost a shell a second, raking the Indian camp, shredding the tepees with flying shrapnel, killing men, women, and children.

"We tried to run," Louise Weasel Bear said, "but they shot us like we were buffalo. I know there are some good white people, but the soldiers must be mean to shoot children and women. Indian soldiers would not do that to white children."

"I was running away from the place and followed those who were running away," said Hakiktawin, another of the young women. "My grandfather and grandmother and brother were killed as we crossed the ravine, and then I was shot on the right hip clear through and on my right wrist where I did not go any further as I was not able to walk, and after the soldier picked me up where a little girl came to me and crawled into the blanket."

When the madness ended, Big Foot and more than half of his people were dead or seriously wounded; 153 were known dead, but many of the wounded crawled away to die afterward. One estimate placed the final total of dead at very nearly three hundred of the original 350 men, women, and children. The soldiers lost twenty-five dead and thirty-nine wounded, most of them struck by their own bullets or shrapnel.

After the wounded cavalrymen were started for the agency at Pine Ridge, a detail of soldiers went over the Wounded Knee battlefield, gathering up Indians who were still alive and loading them into wagons. . . .

The wagonloads of wounded Sioux (four men and forty-seven women and children) reached Pine Ridge after dark. Because all available barracks were filled with soldiers, they were left lying in the open wagons in the bitter cold while an inept Army officer searched for shelter. Finally the Episcopal mission was opened, the benches taken out, and hay scattered over the rough flooring.

It was the fourth day after Christmas in the Year of Our Lord 1890. When the first torn and bleeding bodies were carried into the candlelit church, those who were conscious could see Christmas greenery hanging from the open rafters. Across the chancel front above the pulpit was strung a crudely lettered banner: PEACE ON EARTH, GOOD WILL TO MEN.

Chapter 3

The Disastrous Impact of White Conquest

Whites Exploited Native Cultures and Natural Resources

Wilbur R. Jacobs

In this essay Wilbur R. Jacobs, former professor of history at the University of California, Santa Barbara, examines the often destructive impact that white Americans had on the land and resources of the areas they settled. Fur traders and other pioneers, for example, though often depicted as hearty, God-fearing souls taming an "uncivilized" wilderness, did untold damage by eradicating many animal species. Native American societies, which largely lived in harmony with nature, were an integral part of the frontier environment exploited by whites, Jacobs maintains. In the name of "progress," settlers and developers treated land, resources, and Indians alike, namely as commodities to be utilized, altered, or disposed of. In recent years, he says, white historians have begun to reappraise this chapter of American history, recognizing the mistakes made by whites and the intrinsic worth of the native tribes exploited.

We read in recent news reports that our fish and wildlife are being slaughtered by the thousands. Conservationists warn that many types of birds and animals are in danger of extinction here and abroad as expanding human population relentlessly squeezes them out of wilderness sanctuaries. Even breathing is difficult in air dangerously polluted by millions of automobiles and a huge industrial complex. Many of our lakes and rivers are contaminated, and even our beaches are blackened by sludge washed in from the polluted sea.

The destruction of our natural environment is usually viewed as a great modern problem, the implication being

Reprinted from Wilbur R. Jacobs, *Dispossessing the American Indian: Indians and Whites on the Colonial Frontier* (New York: Scribner's, 1972). Copyright ©1972 by Wilbur R. Jacobs.

that only in the twentieth century has the onslaught taken place. There is a growing realization, however, that from the beginning of our history we Americans have been both destructive and wasteful of natural resources and that the American Indian was an early victim. It is actually the scale of the damage instead of its newness that forces us, though still reluctantly, to confront the problem today.

A Deep Attachment to the Land

We must bear some responsibility for the lateness of our awakening, for we really have not done our homework. We have avoided, and in most cases ignored, the complicated series of historical phenomena that brought about our dilemma. Our histories, particularly our frontier-sectional or "western" histories, tend to give us a glowing get-rich-quick chronicle of the conquest of the continent. As Frederick Jackson Turner wrote in his influential essay of 1893:

> . . . the Indian trade pioneered the way for civilization . . . the trails widened into roads, and the roads into turnpikes, and these in turn were transformed into railroads. . . . In this progress from savage conditions lie topics for the evolutionist.

The Turnerean theme of "progress" of American civilization has generally reflected itself in American social attitudes toward the wilderness. The Indian is viewed as a "consolidating influence" on frontiersmen who banded together for defense. When the tribesman is brought into the story, he is depicted as a kind of obstacle to the westward movement. The Indian's respect for animal life and reverence for the land, when mentioned, are usually dismissed as superstition. On the other hand, the white man, with his Judeo-Christian ethic stressing man's dominance over nature, had no religious scruples about exploiting the wilderness. From the beginning, fur traders, who had rum to encourage warriors to hunt, were often frustrated by the reluctance of natives to busy themselves in the useful activity of scouring the woods for furs and skins. Modern American social attitudes toward wild animals show a persistence of the fur trader's point of view. Unless a species can be fitted into a category of being particularly "useful" in a commercial sense, there is public apathy about its survival. . . .

This strictly utilitarian attitude toward wilderness life, though widespread in American society, has been partially balanced by a counter-theme of wilderness appreciation and respect for the Indian by such writers as Francis Parkman, Henry David Thoreau, John Muir, Willa Cather, and Aldo Leopold. They identified wild country with Indians, with wild animals, and with genuine human freedom. If we have no free-roaming wildlife in wild country, they argued, then we eliminate space for that remaining wild thing, the irrepressible human spirit. These writers particularly felt a kinship for the natural simplicity of the Indian life style that embraced an intuitive understanding of nature's ways. They could appreciate the Indian's deep attachment to lakes, mountains, valleys, and rivers and his ear-to-the-land attitude that is recognized today as the rudiments of ecological awareness. Thoreau in particular could readily sympathize with the "Old People" among the woodland tribes who revered the Mother Earth who had nurtured her people. It was understandable that these agricultural woodland Indians would shun a steel plow that would tear at her body, when it should be gently caressed with a stick or a hoe.

Who Is the Real Varmint?

But the white man's farming and industrial frontiers were based on other principles entirely, bringing about massive alterations in the land. At what point in American history can we say that such carving of the land began to cause ecological changes that would result in permanent damage and hardship for future generations? Do we have an obligation in our histories to criticize harmful white social attitudes about the environment that run contrary to the best interests of the nation at large? . . . Certainly historians have no responsibility for what has happened in the past, but there are historic records showing what earlier generations did or failed to do. Therefore, the public and students can expect writings undistorted by patriotism, prejudice, sentiment, ignorance, or lopsided research. But such a presentation of the

American past is, in certain areas of history, not always the rule. This criticism can be applied particularly to specific topics in "frontier" or "westward movement" history.

Historians of the American frontier, for instance, have failed to impress their readers with the utterly destructive impact that the fur trade had upon the North American continent and the American Indian. There are no investigations of the role the fur men had in killing off certain types of wildlife, which in turn had a permanent effect upon the land and upon native and white societies. The traders and their followers, the fur trading companies, are usually depicted as positive benefactors in the development of American civilization as it moved westward from the Appalachians to the Pacific Coast. The rugged individualistic traits of fur men are praised, in contrast to Indian communal ways in which the hunter killed for his clan or community and not for himself. . . . The historian usually expresses a businessman's outlook in describing the development and expansion of this mercantile enterprise. If the fur trade contributed to the rapid economic growth of the country, and it unquestionably did, then the implication is the fur trade was a good thing for all Americans. Free furs and skins, free land, free minerals—it was all part of the great westward trek and the development of American society, according to Turner and his followers. The self-made man, the heroic figure who conquered the wilderness was the free trapper, the mountain man. . . .

The basic question of interpretation here is: who is the real varmint, the bear or the trapper who killed him? Aside from the fact that bears are sometimes noted for anti-social behavior, our frontier historians have not had a problem in answering such a question because their interpretations have been conditioned by a society steeped in a businessman's ideology. Our view of progress—one that permeates all groups of society and leads us to accept without question the need for an expanding economy—is that progress consists in exploitation and growth, which in turn depends on the commercialization and the conquest of nature. In our histories we have treated the land more as a commodity than as a resource. We have here in a nutshell the *conquistador* [conqueror] mentality that has so long dominated much written American history and relegated the Indian to historical insignificance.

Commercial over National Interests

Until recently historians have ignored the ecological challenge. Yet truthful, interesting American history, double-barreled and difficult to write, is in part the revolting story of how we managed to commercialize all that we could harness and control with our technical skills. It is, in its unvarnished state, an unpleasant narrative of the reckless exploitation of America's Indian people, along with minerals, waterways, soil, timber, wildlife, and wilderness, a part of a larger story of the white man's rape of nature over centuries. Can we ignore the fact that today all Americans can no longer afford such cruelty and wastefulness? . . .

Can modern Americans stand back and look at the historic western migration as a huge page in social history? Can we see how the white man's frontier advance is also the story of the looting and the misuse of land? The traders who led the procession of pioneers through the Cumberland Gap and the South Pass were the vanguard of those who slaughtered wapiti, beaver, buffalo, and antelope and thus reduced the Indian tribes facing the frontier to a state of semi-starvation, making them easy victims for sporadic white military campaigns. Ironically the individual fur men, miners, and cattle raisers were, in many cases, ruined by powerful combines devoted to large-scale commercialization of the natural resources of the West. Because of our exaggerated respect for the entrepreneur (or the pioneer or frontiersman, as we have often called him), we have failed in our histories to condemn this early rape of the land, just as today—and for the same reasons—there is no visible unity behind the condemnation of industrial pollution or the sacrifice of the priceless American wilderness heritage that belongs to all generations of citizens.

How can one assess the historical damage brought about by allowing commercial interests to override our true national interests? A beginning might be an attempt to gauge the effects of the substitution within a half century of hundreds of thousands of horses and domestic cattle for wild hoofed animals that existed in the huge area of the Louisiana Purchase. What effect did this have on the fertility of the land and the ecological balance? Can historians join scientists in calling attention to the important principle that the earth's productivity largely depends upon an organic cycle, an order of nature in which organic material taken from the earth must be returned to it? The ignorance of this principle by white Americans in the eighteenth and nineteenth centuries was responsible for the destruction of the ecosystems of a great virgin wilderness. In this destruction the substitution of annual grasses for the life-sustaining primordial prairie sod of middle America is one of the more momentous happenings in American history, but the subject is something less than a favorite with historians of the frontier. We know, for example, that in Texas huge prairie grasslands have been converted into a mesquite jungle resulting from overgrazing and fencing a land that had once been burned periodically by Indians and by some stockmen who followed their example. Today, only along railroad rights of way is there preserved the ancient prairie flora that has survived many burnings. We may soon learn to appreciate the fact that the Indian is closely tied to the ecological history of the American nation and opposition to the pioneer's changing the face of the land. . . .

The Dismal Story of Mass Slaughter

It can be argued that we cannot morally condemn our pioneers for exploitation. They acted in a manner consistent with their circumstances, within their concepts of territorial rights, justice, and morality. Their actions were governed by needs and impulses that differed in about as many ways from those of their neighbors in the frontier behind them as from those of their Indian foes in the wild land before them. When the sky was darkened by thousands of pigeons, the normal expected reaction was to kill them off wastefully. What we can blame is the continuation of such attitudes into an era of scarcity. We should understand our pioneers, perhaps, rather than blaming them for what they did.

It can be further argued that the pioneers, who were quite as mercenary as the leaders of large companies and early corporations, did not understand the long-range consequences of what they were doing to the land. There were few individuals among the farmers, the hydraulic strip and dredge miners, the loggers, or the sheep and cattle men—or for that matter, the fur companies and the railroad tycoons—who had any real conception of the vital importance of the resources they were destroying. They did not grasp the significance of muddy streams (caused by the clear-cutting of forests) that had once run deep and clear. Nor did they appreciate the importance of the vital prairie grasses that were plowed under in a few decades. They were often unaware that precious minerals quickly and forever disappeared from our streams and mountains. Indeed, what nineteenth century conservationists complained about the railroads destroying the ecological balance of the Great Plains?

Yet it is not entirely true that the pioneers, the miners, the fur men, and the western entrepreneurs were ignorant of the consequences of their acts. The pioneer's question, "Why should I look after my descendants?" and his answer, "They ain't done nothin' for me," go back generations in American history. Nor were the Indians allowed to stand in the way when there were valuable land assets to be developed by white frontier society. In California, for example, the manner and thoroughness in which California's wildlife and groups of aboriginal people were killed or exploited is a mark against all Americans. The Spaniards and Mexicans of California were evidently able to live with wildlife without destroying it. But the forty-niners of California's golden age and their followers were wildly wasteful of elk, antelope, bighorns, bears, small fur-bearing animals, grouse, geese, and shorebirds. Thousands of dollars were made by selling game meat to miners. In California alone a great faunal shift took place in the years 1850–1910, duplicated only by prehistoric postglacial terminations of certain species. The California grizzly was pursued until none at all survive today. Here we have a historic example of the dismal story of mass slaughter of wildlife. . . .

Indian Land Wisdom

Henry David Thoreau, as much as any other writer of the nineteenth century, perceived that the white man misunderstood the woodland Indian. Our histories, Thoreau was convinced, were full of prejudice and misconceptions. Writing in his journal in 1859 he argued that the portrayal of "the Indians, as a race possessing so little skill and wit, so low in the scale of humanity, and so brutish that they hardly deserved to be remembered," did primitive men an injustice. "It frequently happens that the historian," commented Thoreau, "though he professes more humanity than the trapper . . . [who] shoots one as a wild beast, really exhibits and practices a similar inhumanity to him, wielding a pen instead of a rifle." Thoreau believed that when the history of primitive peoples is written by men convinced of the superiority of their own race, then it is no history at all, for it deprives us of a knowledge of what kind of men the natives were and how they lived, "their relation to nature, their arts and their customs, their fancies and superstitions . . . beliefs connected with the sea and forest which," he argued, "concern us quite as much as the fables of oriental nations do." Thoreau recognized almost instinctively that primitive peoples the world over have much in common, especially in their closeness to nature and their remarkable ability to adapt their lives to their physical environment. "The thought of a so-called savage tribe," he concluded, "is generally far more just than that of a single civilized man." Our most recent scholars of the American Indian would find it hard to disagree.

White America may not wish to acknowledge it, but a part of our modern ecological awareness can certainly be traced to the historic land wisdom of the Indian, a heritage of all Americans. If our "progress" has all but overwhelmed the Indian, it can be seen in the litter, paint spray, and aluminum cans that today decorate portions of what was once a pristine Navajo land. Willa Cather some fifty years ago recorded for posterity the ancient Navajo practice of "leave no trace" on the land in her novel *Death Comes for the Archbishop:*

When they left the rock or tree or sand dune that had sheltered them for the night, the Navajo was careful to obliterate every trace of their temporary occupation. He buried the embers of the fire and the remnants of food, unpiled any stones he had piled together, filled up the holes he had scooped in the sand. Since this was Jacinto's procedure, Father Latour judged that, just as it was the white man's way to assert himself in any landscape, to change it, make it over a little (at least to leave some mark or memorial of his sojourn), it was the Indian's way to pass through a country without disturbing anything; to pass and leave no trace, like fish through the water, or birds through the air. It was the Indian manner to vanish into the landscape, not to stand out against it. . . . [Indians] seemed to have none of the European's desire to "master" nature, to arrange and recreate. They spent their ingenuity in another direction, in accommodating themselves to the scene in which they found themselves.

Dehumanizing the Indian

The white man could never adapt himself to the idea that he would "vanish into the landscape" as the Indian quietly did. Where does the balance lie, and how may modern U.S. society evaluate the Indian's unique contribution to the American historical perspective? Surely the non-Indian may learn much from Indian cultural affinity with nature just as the Indian has profited from some scientific advances of white technology. Today it is abundantly evident that our history is barren in the sense that it needs to bolster itself with more about Indians (as well as other minorities) and their way of life. Modern America, the swirling product of a long historical development, is increasingly mechanized, polluted, and depersonalized and has a disturbing tendency toward beehive regimentation. Can such a society help but profit from having better understanding of the Indian's historic reverence for the land and his humane lifestyle? In fact, isn't it almost self-evident that we desperately need the native American Indian and his culture? Perhaps when our histories at last reconcile the white man's great accomplishments with a true appreciation of what the Indian considered the virtues of Mother Earth, we may then have redirected our priorities toward an unpolluted, pluralistic society that will prosper "as long as the rivers shall run and the grass shall grow." Like the Indian we may learn that it is almost impossible to separate the materialistic side of conservation from the spiritual and subjective aspects of life itself. Perhaps the tragedy coming out of our frontier-*conquistador* myth is the general acceptance of the idea that our pioneering civilization, with its great Judaic-Christian heritage (GOOD), conquered a wilderness peopled by savage, pagan Indians (EVIL). Our Christian pioneers who revered their spirits in a trinity rather than in rocks, plants, and beasts, came to regard their conquered opponents as nonpersons. In dehumanizing the Indian, however, they almost unavoidably dehumanized themselves as they chopped, hunted, tilled, and mined on a virgin land that had once belonged to a native people.

The Tactics and Impact of Indian Removal and Relocation

Peter Farb

One of the most devastating aspects of the American Indian wars was the forced removal of whole tribes from their ancestral lands and relocation to distant, often inhospitable regions. In this essay, Peter Farb, former curator of American Indian Cultures at the Riverside Museum in New York City, effectively explains the rationale and methods employed by whites during Indian removal. He then examines the horrendous impact removal and relocation had on Native American cultures, paying special attention to the sad plight of the Cherokee, whose suffering was particularly extreme.

Following the War of 1812, the young United States had no further need for Indian allies against the British, and as a result the fortunes of the Indians declined rapidly. By 1848, twelve new states had been carved out of the Indians' lands, two major and many minor Indian wars had been fought, and group after group of Indians had been herded westward, on forced marches, across the Mississippi River.

The 1830 Removal Act

As in other inhumane and deceitful chapters in the history of the United States, the justifications of God and civilization were invoked. To Senator Thomas Hart Benton of Missouri it was all very simple: The Whites must supplant Indians because Whites used the land "according to the intentions of the Creator." Some spoke of the benefits to the Indian of removing him from contact with Whites, which would give him the time to assimilate at his own pace the blessings of civilization. A senator from Georgia, hoping to expedite the removal of Indians from his state to what later became Oklahoma, glowingly described that arid, treeless territory as a place "over which Flora has scattered her beauties with a wanton hand; and upon whose bosom innumerable wild animals display their amazing numbers."

Such statements do not mean that the Indians lacked defenders, but the intensity of the indignation was in direct proportion to a White's distance from the Indian. On the frontier, the Indian was regarded as a besotted savage; but along the eastern seaboard, where the Spaniards, Dutch, English, and later the Americans had long since exterminated almost all the Indians, philosophers and divines began to defend the Red Man. In response to Georgia's extirpation [uprooting] of her Indian population, Ralph Waldo Emerson protested: "The soul of man, the justice, the mercy that is the heart's heart in all men, from Maine to Georgia, does abhor this business." Presidents such as Jefferson, Monroe, and Adams, who came from the East, occasionally displayed some scruples about the treatment the Indian was receiving. . . .

But President Andrew Jackson had been reared on the frontier and he was utterly insensitive to the treatment of the Indians. He denounced as an "absurdity" and a "farce" that the United States should bother even to negotiate treaties with Indians as if they were independent nations with a right to their lands. He was completely in sympathy with the policy of removal of the Indians to new lands west of the Mississippi. He exerted his influence to make Congress give legal sanction to what in our own time, under the Nuremburg Laws, would be branded as genocide. Dutifully, Congress passed the Removal Act of 1830, which gave the President the right to extirpate all Indians who had managed to survive east of the Mississippi River. It was estimated that the whole job might be done economically at no more than $500,000—the costs to be kept low by persuasion, promises, threats, and the bribery of Indian leaders. When U.S. Supreme Court Justice John Marshall ruled in favor of the Cherokee in a case with wide implications for protecting the

Indians, Jackson is said to have remarked: "John Marshall has made his decision, now let him enforce it."

Becoming Historical Footnotes

During the next ten years, almost all the Indians were cleared from the East. Some like the Chickasaw and Choctaw went resignedly, but many others left only at bayonet point. The Seminole actively resisted and some retreated into the Florida swamps, where they stubbornly held off the United States Army. The Seminole Wars lasted from 1835 to 1842 and cost the United States some 1,500 soldiers and an estimated $20,000,000 (about forty times what Jackson had estimated it would cost to remove all Indians). Many of the Iroquois sought sanctuary in Canada, and the Oneida and the Seneca were moved westward, although fragments of Iroquois tribes managed to remain behind in western New York. The Sac and Fox made a desperate stand in Illinois against overwhelming numbers of Whites, but ultimately their survivors also were forced to move, as were the Ottawa, Potawatomie, Wyandot, Shawnee, Kickapoo, Winnebago, Delaware, Peoria, Miami, and many others who are remembered now only in the name of some town, lake, county, or state, or as a footnote in the annals of a local historical society.

All in all, an estimated seventy thousand Indians are believed to have been resettled west of the Mississippi, but the number may have been closer to one hundred thousand. No figures exist, though, as to the numbers massacred before they could be persuaded to leave the East, or on the tremendous losses suffered from disease, exposure, and starvation on the thousand-mile march westward across an unsettled and inhospitable land.

The "Civilized" Cherokee

Some of the Indians who were forced west of the Mississippi might with justification be regarded as "savages," but this cannot be said of the Cherokee. About 1790 the Cherokee decided to adopt the ways of their White conquerors and to emulate their civilization, their morals, their learning, and their arts. The Cherokee made remarkable and rapid progress in their homeland in the mountains where Georgia, Tennessee, and North Carolina meet. They established churches, mills, schools, and well-cultivated farms; judging from descriptions of that time, the region was a paradise when compared with the bleak landscape that the White successors have made of Appalachia today. In 1826 a Cherokee reported to the Presbyterian Church that his people already possessed 22,000 cattle, 7,600 houses, 46,000 swine, 2,500 sheep, 762 looms, 1,488 spinning wheels, 2,948 plows, 10 saw mills, 31 grist mills, 62 blacksmith shops, and 18 schools. In one of the Cherokee districts alone there were some 1,000 volumes "of good books." In 1821, after twelve years of hard work, a Cherokee named Sequoya (honored in the scientific names for the redwood and the giant sequoia trees in California, three thousand miles from his homeland) perfected a method of syllabary notation in which English letters stood for Cherokee syllables; by 1828 the Cherokee were already publishing their own newspaper. At about the same time, they adopted a written constitution providing for an executive, a bicameral legislature, a supreme court, and a code of laws.

Before the passage of the Removal Act of 1830, a group of Cherokee chiefs went to the Senate committee that was studying this legislation, to report on what they had already achieved in the short space of forty years. They expressed the hope that they would be permitted to enjoy in peace "the blessings of civilization and Christianity on the soil of their rightful inheritance." Instead, they were daily subjected to brutalities and atrocities by White neighbors, harassed by the state government of Georgia, cajoled and bribed by federal agents to agree to removal, and denied even the basic protection of the federal government. Finally, in 1835, a minority faction of five hundred Cherokee out of a total of some twenty thousand signed a treaty agreeing to removal. The Removal Act was carried out almost everywhere with a notable lack of compassion, but in the case of the Cherokee—civilized and Christianized as they were—it was particularly brutal.

After many threats, about five thousand finally consented to be marched westward, but another fifteen thousand clung to their neat farms, schools, and libraries "of good books." So General Winfield Scott set about systematically extirpating the rebellious ones. Squads of soldiers descended upon isolated Cherokee farms and at bayonet point marched the families off to what today would be known as concentration camps. Torn from their homes with all the dispatch and efficiency the Nazis displayed under similar circumstances, the families had no time to prepare for the arduous trip ahead of them. No way existed for the Cherokee family to sell its property and possessions, and the local Whites fell upon the lands, looting, burning, and finally taking possession.

Some Cherokee managed to escape into the gorges and thick forests of the Great Smoky Mountains, where they became the nucleus of those living there today, but most were finally rounded up or killed. They then were set off on a thousand-mile march—called to this day "the trail of tears" by the Cherokee—that was one of the notable death marches in history. Ill clad, badly fed, lacking medical attention, and prodded on by soldiers wielding bayonets, the Indians suffered severe losses. An estimate made at the time stated that some four thousand Cherokee died en route, but that figure is certainly too low. At the very moment that these people were dying in droves, President Van Buren reported to Congress that the government's handling of the Indian problem had been "just and friendly throughout; its efforts for their civilization constant, and directed by the best feelings of humanity; its watchfulness in protecting them from individual frauds unremitting." Such cynicism at the highest level of government has been approached in our own time by the solemn pronouncements by President Lyndon B. Johnson about the Vietnam War.

Their Nation Has Ceased to Exist

One man who examined the young United States with a perceptive eye and who wrote it all down in his *Democracy in America*, [Frenchman] Alexis de Tocqueville, happened to be in Memphis during an unusually cold winter when the thermometer hovered near zero. There he saw a ragged party of docile Choctaw, part of the thousands who had reluctantly agreed to be transported to the new lands in the western part of what was then the Arkansas Territory. Wrote de Tocqueville:

> It was then the middle of winter, and the cold was unusually severe; the snow had frozen hard upon the ground and the river was drifting huge masses of ice. The Indians had their families with them, and they brought in their train the wounded and the sick, with children newly born and old men upon the verge of death. They possessed neither tents nor wagons, but only their arms and some provisions. I saw them embark to pass the mighty river, and never will that solemn spectacle fade from my remembrance. No cry, no sob, was heard among the assembled crowd; all was silent. Their calamities were of ancient date, and they knew them to be irremediable.

De Tocqueville was a discerning observer of the methods used by the Americans to deal with the Indians, and he described with restrained outrage how the Indians were sent westward by government agents: ". . . half convinced and half compelled, they go to inhabit new deserts, where the importunate whites will not let them remain ten years in peace. In this manner do the Americans obtain, at a very low price, whole provinces, which the richest sovereigns of Europe could not purchase." Reporting that a mere 6,273 Indians still survived in the thirteen original states, he predicted accurately the fate of the Indians in their new homes across the Mississippi:

> The countries to which the newcomers betake themselves are inhabited by other tribes, which receive them with jealous hostility. Hunger is in the rear, war awaits them, and misery besets them on all sides. To escape from so many enemies, they separate, and each individual endeavors to procure secretly the means of supporting his existence.

Long before the science of anthropology and the study of what today is politely called "culture change," de Tocqueville understood how an entire culture might become raveled like some complexly woven fabric:

> The social tie, which distress had long since weakened, is
> then dissolved; they have no longer a country, and soon they
> will not be a people; their very families are obliterated; their
> common name is forgotten; their language perishes; and all
> traces of their origin disappear. Their nation has ceased to
> exist except in the recollections of the antiquaries of America
> and a few of the learned of Europe.

Indian Pitted Against Indian

The great removal was not the panacea that its advocates in
Congress had maintained, in the names of God and civilization, it would be. Families had been separated, and many Indians had died en route. The new lands were much less hospitable to farming than those the Indians had been forced to
evacuate, and the different game animals required new skills
to hunt. To make matters worse, there was the hostility of the
Plains Indians, who had been inveigled [enticed] into giving
up some of their lands to make room for the eastern Indians.
The Plains Indians asserted that the bison had been driven
away by the newcomers, and clashes between various groups
became increasingly common. The Chickasaw, who had dutifully agreed to removal, said they could not take up the land
assigned to them because of their fear of the "wild tribes" already inhabiting it. The United States government no more
honored its obligation to protect the Indians in their new
territory than it had honored any of its previous obligations
toward them. In 1834 fewer than three thousand troops were
available along the entire frontier to maintain order and to
protect the newcomers against the Plains tribes. The result
was that the very Indians whose removal had been ordered
ostensibly to pacify and to civilize them were forced once
more to take up their old warrior ways to defend themselves.
So the result of the great removal was that once again, as in
earlier years of competition between French and English, Indian was pitted against Indian for the benefit of the Whites.

Slaughter of the Buffalo, Livelihood of the Plains Tribes

Stephen Longstreet

Often, after a tribe had been robbed of its lands and relocated, it became exceedingly difficult for its members to sustain themselves. This was especially true of the Plains Indians, who depended on the buffalo for food, clothing, and other means of subsistence. In a the span of just a few decades, thousands of white hunters decimated the great buffalo herds that had once roamed the western plains. Worse, the hunters regularly and wantonly plied their trade on the recently formed Indians reservations, soon leaving many tribes nearly destitute. This spirited examination of buffalo hunters and Indians is by Stephen Longstreet, a noted historian, journalist, and teacher. He ends his narrative with a description of a battle in which some Indians tried to stop a group of hunters from killing the last of their buffalo. Faced with the superior firepower of the buffalo guns, the Indians failed in their mission, several of their number dying in the process. This scene, repeated with slight variations across the western frontier, effectively emphasizes the futility of Native American attempts to stop the advance of white civilization.

The decline of the buffalo herds was the ultimate tragedy for the Indians of the Plains. Without buffalo, they starved. They had little else to hunt. Lost was the source for food, clothing, tepee covering, gear made of buffalo fur and hide. The buffalo was tasty eating: his hump a gourmet's delight and the gut, slightly singed, much prized. It was almost impossible for an Indian raised on buffalo meat to eat the stringy, tasteless steers

Reprinted from *War Cries on Horseback: The Story of the Indian Wars of the Great Plains*, by Stephen Longstreet (New York: W.H. Allen, 1971). Copyright ©1970 by Stephen Longstreet.

the agency provided for him on the reservations and he got few enough of those from a dishonest agent. Most officials were indifferent to the Indian, except as a means of making a trader or agent rich. Bull boats, sleeping robes, saddles, belting, parfleche [untanned hide used to make arrow quivers and other items], pouches—all were best made from buffalo hide. Jerked buffalo meat, sun-dried or smoked, carried the red man over a hard winter. Buffalo chip—the dried dung—made fine fires on a treeless plain. Now the great herds were fading away.

Shooters and Skinners

The white men were not just thinning the herds; they were exterminating them in their greed for pelts. Buffalo hunters left hundreds of thousands, then millions of carcasses to rot away unused, wasting vital food and abolishing all the other useful purposes the Indian might have realized.

A hide-hunter was interested only in cash value of hides; he didn't give a damn for the Indians' needs. A hide-hunting outfit with skinners could kill hundreds of buffalo in one day and the slaughter never let up. The hunters were armed with a deadly weapon—a Buffalo gun; actually, the Sharps .50-calibre, sending a 600-grain of lead shot backed by 125 grains of powder, for the kill. Heavy and long-bored, the Sharps rifle was deadly in the hands of an expert shot. Buffalo have poor eyesight and a hide-hunter on the right side of the wind could kill an entire herd while they grazed one by one without stampeding them. Thousands of buffalo hunters stalked the migrations.

The skinner was a skilled specialist. Two skinners with a team of horses—speedy workers—slit the skin of the bison belly and up the legs; then, hitching one end of the skin to the team, the horses were driven forward to peel off the hide. Bales of hides packed every railhead—40,000 accumulated some days at Dodge City. Prices fell as more hunters appeared—hides going from five dollars each to four bits (a half dollar). In two years (from 1872 to 1874) when some sort of company records were kept, the railroads shipped out a million and a half hides and nearly seven million pounds of buffalo tongues and hams.

Besides this, the railroad meat killers slaughtered thousands of buffalo to feed their workers. William Cody was such a meat hunter for the Goddard Brothers, who fed the construction crews of the Kansas-Pacific Railroad. In seven months he killed 4280 buffalo on the job. He was a feckless frontier drunkard but a handsome figure of a man with his fringed buckskins, long blond hair, and courtly goatee.

A journalist who called himself Ned Buntline labeled him Buffalo Bill and wrote a set of invented adventures about him. In this long series of dime novels, Cody was a great Indian killer, too. Actually, Army records show he was once a scout with the 5th Cavalry and that he had ridden for the Pony Express. Two quarts of whisky was his daily dosage if he could get it and mostly, he could. Of all the buffalo killers, Cody became the most famous.

The Ground Seemed to Tremble

For a truer picture of the buffalo slaughter, one can turn to the memories of Robert Wright who hunted, killed, and shipped buffalo pelts for fifteen years from the buffalo Plains country. He knew the buffalo when, as he says, it was impossible to count them. "I have traveled through a herd of them days and days, never out of sight of them; in fact, it might be correctly called one continuous gathering of the great shaggy monsters.

"I have been present at many a cattle roundup and have seen ten-thousand head in one herd and under complete control of their drivers; but I have seen herds of buffalo so immense in number that the vast aggregation of domestic cattle seemed as nothing at all compared with them. The southwestern plains, in early days, was the greatest country on earth and the buffalo was the noblest as well as the most plentiful of the game animals. I have, indeed, traveled through buffaloes along the Arkansas River for two-hundred miles, almost one continuous herd as close together as it is customary to herd cattle. You might go north or south as far as you pleased and there would seem no diminution of their numbers. When they were suddenly frightened and stampeded, they made a roar like thunder and the ground seemed to tremble. When, after nightfall, they came to the river, particularly when it was in flood, their immense numbers in their headlong plunge would make you think, by the thunderous noise, that they had dashed all the water from the river. They often went without water one and two days in summer and much longer in winter. No one had any idea of their numbers.

"General Sheridan and Major Inman were at Fort Dodge one night, having just made the trip from Fort Supply, and called me in to consult as to how many buffaloes there were between Dodge and Supply. Taking a strip fifty miles east and fifty miles west, they had first made it ten billion. General Sheridan said, 'That number don't do.' They figured it again, and made it one billion. Finally they reached the conclusion that there must be one-hundred billion, but said they were afraid to give out these figures; nevertheless, they believed them. This vast herd moved slowly toward the north when spring opened, and moved steadily back again from the far north when the days began to grow short and winter was settling in.

Time Has Proved the Indians Correct

"Horace Greeley estimated the number of buffaloes at five million. I agree with him, only I think there were nearly five times that number. I lived in the heart of the buffalo range for nearly fifteen years.

"I am told that some recent writer who has studied the buffalo closely has placed their number at ninety million and I think that he is nearer right than I. Brick Bond, a resident of Dodge—an old, experienced hunter, a great shot, and a most reliable man as to . . . honesty says that he killed fifteen hundred buffaloes in seven days and his highest killing was two-hundred and fifty in one day, and he had to be on the lookout for hostile Indians all the time. He had fifteen skinners, and he was only one of many hunters.

"Charles Rath and I shipped over two-hundred thousand buffalo hides the first winter the Atchison, Topeka and Santa Fe Railroad reached Dodge City and I think there were at least as many more shipped from there, besides two hundred

cars of hind-quarters and two cars of buffalo tongues. Often
have I shot them from the walls of my corral, for my hogs to
feed upon. Several times, I have seen wagon-trains stop to
let the immense herds pass; besides, many of them,
wounded, would wander off, out of sight and reach, and
were not found until they were unfit for market; and the Indians claimed that the noise of the hunters' guns and their
mode of killing would soon drive the buffalo out of the
country or annihilate them. Time has proved that the Indians were correct.

"A band of hunters cared no more for Indians than Indians did for foot-soldiers and, unless they greatly outnumbered the hunters—and then only under the most favorable
circumstances—the Indians would not attack the hunters.
They were afraid of the hunter's big guns, his cool bravery
and, last but not least, of his unerring, deadly aim. Then,
too, the hunter had but little plunder that was dear to the Indian, after the fight was won—only a team of work-horses
and the redskin cared much more for riding ponies than for
work animals.". . .

Some Indians Strike Back

When the herds were devastated, the bone collectors came
to pile up mountains of skulls and other bones of the dead
bison, to ship them east to be ground into fertilizer.

By 1875, the hide business was almost finished and no one
bothered to keep any records of the killings. Nearly every
eastern family that could afford one had a buffalo robe or
two and, for a little while, there were buffalo coats.

The loss of the herds, as much as the greed of land grab-
bers and gold hunters and the continuous battles with the
soldiers, signaled the coming of the end of the Indian way of
life. The Indian treaties, pledged to leave some buffalo lands
to the tribes, were not honored. As buffalo disappeared in
the northern Plains, hide hunters invaded Indian lands in the
Texas Panhandle. Teams of shooters and skinners, busy at
their trade, were everywhere.

There was in 1874 an old, old adobe ruin in the Texas Panhandle on Bent Creek, of a Bent and St. Vrain trading post,

called Adobe Walls. Hide men from Dodge City built a fort there: stores, saloon; hide buyers and dealers were housed. Some scouts reported seeing Indian signs, but the hide hunters and skinners went on hauling back great loads of hides to the Walls—predatory and destructive as ever. A hunter named Plummer, bringing hides to his lonely camp one day found his two partners killed and scalped, one with a stake driven through his heart. Plummer recognized the desolation and danger and rode hard for the fort. Two other hunters were killed at the Salt Fork of the Red River. The Indians were on the war path against the hide men. The hunters collected at Adobe Walls, shaking their heads at the situation. Night fell, heat lightning sawed the sky and, in the brush all around, desert owls hooted. The fort turned in to get some sleep: twenty-eight men and the wife of the owner of the eating place. Most of the hunters slept outside, on the ground, as the night was a scorcher. The horses were nervous in the heat and the lightning flashing on the horizon. In the Hanrahan Saloon at the fort—a building made up of piled-up sod held upon a cottonwood ridgepole—the pole suddenly broke, with a great crash. This woke everyone, to curses and laughter. Nobody slept any more. The roof was repaired at dawn.

Battle at Adobe Walls

A hunter named Billy Dixon went down to saddle his pony and went bug-eyed as he saw coming out of the woods a huge band of Indians, all in their war paint and feathers, whipping up their ponies. They saw Dixon and gave out their war cries. Dixon mounted and rode for the fort, shouting the alarm: "Injuns!"

The buffalo hunters and fort people grabbed rifles as the Indians charged right for the buildings, their howling growing more shrill in pitch. These were Cheyenne, horrifying to see, all garbed and smeared for war with lances, shields, and war bonnets. They came in a rush straight to the attack without dallying or prancing about. Two brothers, the Shadlers, sleeping in a wagon outside the fort, were killed at once. The charge came fast, overrunning the fort, massing between the buildings which were full of whites. The hunters were divided. Nine men were in the saloon among the whisky kegs. They were short of ammunition. Eleven men were in one store; six others with the woman, Mrs. Olds, were in the other. Windows were shattered, rifle and lance butts beat at the barred doors. The killing of Indians by skilled crack-shot hunters had begun. Wounded bucks scrambled for safety as the attackers suddenly withdrew.

The Indians tried a shooting match but the buffalo hunters' heavier guns outmatched them. . . .

One of the white hunters was shot as he stepped outdoors for a better shot, and that encouraged the Indians to make another charge. The charge failed, but Indians began to pile up behind buffalo-robe bales in the stockade for close shooting. . . .

By four o'clock, the Indian fire died out and the survivors looked at one another with wonder. Some fool stepped out to see what was up and no one fired. The Cheyenne had pulled out, impressed by the deadly fire of the hide hunters. Nearby were thirteen dead Indians, but it was unsafe for their friends to go in to retrieve the bodies. There were fifty-six dead Indian ponies lying around. The hide hunters, in jubilation, claimed they'd killed nearly a hundred hostiles. The Indian official report was: nine Cheyenne and Comanche killed, which was fewer than the thirteen dead left beside the walls. . . .

The excitement in the fort was not over. William Olds, whose wife had been the only woman in the fort, was killed by his own rifle while getting down from a ladder. Two days later, the dust column of a Dodge City relief company appeared on the horizon, and the battle and siege of Adobe Walls was over.

Indian Cultures Decimated by Alcoholism and Disease

Brian W. Dippie

White settlers and soldiers did more than dispossess Native Americans of their lands, means of subsistence, and human rights. They also introduced alcohol and Old World diseases to the Indians, causing tremendous social disruption, suffering, and death. Brian W. Dippie of the history department at the University of Victoria, British Columbia, here summarizes the effects of alcoholism on Native American cultures, explaining that white scholars long held that Indians must be "biologically disposed" to drunkenness. He also discusses Indian tolls brought about by white diseases, zeroing in on one of the most deadly— smallpox, which nearly wiped out several tribes.

For the Indians, alcohol brought with it a whole train of destructive consequences—quarrels disruptive of family and social life, the breakdown of traditional moral sanctions, impaired health due to exposure during bouts of drinking, maiming, prostitution, venereal disease, murder, and a lowered birth rate. A Jesuit priest in Canada in 1637 informed his superior that the rising number of deaths among the natives "is attributed to the beverages of brandy and wine, which they love with an utterly unrestrained passion, not for the relish they experience in drinking them, but for the pleasure they find in becoming drunk. . . . As they drink without eating, and in great excess, I can easily believe that the maladies which are daily tending to exterminate them, may in part arise from that." Tribal leaders over the centuries have struggled with the effects of intoxicating liquors on their people, and the phenomenon of Indian alcohol addiction—characterized by a pattern of compulsive or pathological drinking—has inspired an extensive professional literature. In the 1970s, scientists at the Oklahoma Center for Alcohol-Related Research entered a thorny area of controversy by suggesting that Indians might have a genetic intolerance to distilled spirits; two Canadians pointed to the possibility that hypoglycemia, exacerbated by severe stress and nutritional deficiencies, accounts for the Indian's susceptibility to strong drink; while an anthropologist, discounting physiological explanations in favor of the notion of cultural determination, argued that Indian drinking is an assertion of Indianness before an indifferent or hostile world.

Drunkenness a Racial Defect?

In the early nineteenth century, however, Indian drunkenness was explained away as just another of those providential causes operating to clear the path for civilization. "The inordinate indulgence of the Indians in spirituous liquors is one of the most deplorable consequences, which has resulted from their intercourse with civilized men," Lewis Cass wrote in 1827. Governor of Michigan Territory from 1813 to 1831, Secretary of War under Andrew Jackson, Secretary of State under James Buchanan, and himself the unsuccessful Democratic candidate for the presidency in 1848, Cass made his original reputation as a man of action leading an Ohio volunteer regiment and then a regular army brigade against the British in the northwestern theater of the War of 1812. As a self-confessed authority on the American Indian ("I know the Indians thoroughly," he advised George Catlin [a famous painter and writer who recorded Indian life]), Cass was one of those nineteenth-century Americans regarded by their contemporaries as "Indian experts." He exerted weighty influence on the nation's Indian policy, and his views, advanced between 1826 and 1830 in a series of articles in the *North American Review*, were always given an attentive hearing.

Though Cass properly deplored the effects of alcohol on the Indian, he felt that the problem went deeper than strong drink. "Among other nations, civilized and barbarous, excessive ebriety [drunkenness] is an individual characteristic, sometimes indulged and sometimes avoided," he observed. "But the Indians in immediate contact with our settlements, old and young, male and female, the chief and the warrior, all give themselves up to the most brutal intoxication, whenever this mad water can be procured." The Indian's alcoholism was, in effect, biologically induced, his extremely low resistance proof of some racial defect ("a national idiosyncracy," Cass would much later term it).

Give Us the Whiskey

Drunkenness was, in microcosm, the entire Indian problem: upon contact with the white race, the Indian exchanged his virtues for civilized vices. Against these vices the Indian had no defense. The government, try as it might to stanch the flow of spirits into Indian country, was doomed to failure. The Indian *wanted* liquor. Cass remembered how a venerable chief of the Potawatomies, during the negotiations at the Treaty of Chicago in 1821, begged the commissioners to give his people alcohol, saying, "Father, we care not for the money, nor the land, nor the goods. We want the whiskey. Give us the whiskey." The traders competed to satisfy the Indian's craving. "Little does the spirit of commerce care how many Indians die inebriates, if it can be assured of beaver skins," Henry Schoolcraft, Cass's friend and himself a recognized Indian expert, lamented in 1829. Laws and regulations alone could not stop the flow of liquor into Indian country. The government might as well attempt to arrest the law of civilized progress, for Indian drunkenness was its direct result. Cass did remark that the "revolting scenes" of Indian drunkenness were fortunately "confined to the vicinity of the settlements, where spirituous liquors can be more easily procured." Indians remote from the settlements were still innocent of alcohol. At a time when the government was pondering a general policy of removing the eastern tribes west of the Mississippi, far away from white society, Cass's remarks were of more than casual interest.

Modern authorities who favor a high estimate of pre-Columbian [i.e., before Columbus's arrival in 1492] Indian numbers have consistently maintained that "disease in epidemic form" was "the greatest factor in [native] depopulation." If we accept a hemispheric estimate of 50 to 75 million population (such as was advanced by [scholar] H.J. Spinden at a time when the orthodox figure was 7 to 10 million), or the even higher projection of Henry F. Dobyns [another scholar] of between 90 and 112.5 million, only devastating epidemics, Dobyns has argued, can explain such "tremendous mortality."

Since the Pilgrims arrived to find that a "wasting plague" introduced earlier probably by English traders had nearly wiped out the local native population, Anglo-Saxons were aware of the deadly effects of their own diseases imparted to the New World natives. The devastation they suffered only fortified the suspicion that they were constitutionally inferior or "feeble." Civilization was to advance with a minimum of resistance, and disease was to be its cutting edge. "The vast preparations for the protection of the western frontier are superfluous," an observer wrote in 1838 after smallpox had raged among the western tribes. "Another arm has undertaken the defense of the white inhabitants of the frontier; and the funeral torch, that lights the red man to his dreary grave, has become the auspicious star of the advancing settler, and of the roving trader of the white race."

The Smallpox Vaccine

Smallpox epidemics, occurring among the tribes with increasing frequency as the eighteenth century neared its end, doubtless helped usher in the full-blown theory of the Vanishing American in the second decade of the nineteenth century. With Edward Jenner's discovery in 1797 that a cowpox culture would safely and effectively immunize humans against smallpox, all-out vaccination programs were urged as the Indian's one hope for survival, and became government policy after an epidemic in 1831–1832 decimated the Pawnees and other tribes along the Platte River. The western tribes remained highly suspicious of vaccination, while they were healthy, turning to it only as a last, belated resort. As a consequence a series of epidemics between 1836 and

1840 ravaged tribes along the West Coast from Alaska to California, and swept across the Southwest. A particularly virulent [deadly] epidemic devastated the Upper Missouri tribes in 1837, nearly annihilating the Mandans before racing upriver as far as the country of the Blackfoot.

Deserted Villages

Although thousands of Indians in every afflicted area perished, the virtual extinction of the Mandans, a well-known, sedentary people, most profoundly impressed contemporary observers. Both Catlin and [Henry R.] Schoolcraft [a noted scholar who recorded Indian languages and customs] regarded the destruction of the Mandans as symbolic of the Indian's fate. With a measure of foresight, Catlin had paid particular attention to the Mandans on his trip to the West in 1832. With a measure of hindsight (since his letters from the Indian country did not appear in book form until 1841, permitting ample time for selective revision), he observed that they were a "strange, yet kind and hospitable, people, whose fate, like that of all their race, is sealed; whose doom is fixed to live just long enough to be imperfectly known, and then to fall before the fell disease or sword of civilizing devastation." Prophecy or not, the remark was unerringly accurate. Schoolcraft, in turn, rated smallpox, "scourge to the aborigines," just below "ardent spirits" as a cause of Indian decline. He recorded incidents arising from the epidemic of 1837, including the attempts to warn other tribes of the danger after the Mandans were infected. The tribe was reduced from 1,600 to 31 souls, Schoolcraft wrote; the Minnetarees, Arickarees, Assiniboines, Crows, and Blackfeet all suffered heavy losses. Granting everything that could be asked on the "score of excitement and exaggeration," he concluded that not fewer than 10,000 Indians (Catlin had suggested 25,000, exclusive of the Mandans) perished of the disease in a matter of weeks. Villages deserted by the fleeing tribes were left inhabited only by a few stray wolves "fattening on the human carcasses that [lay] strewed about."

The government, as Catlin pointed out, had made "repeated efforts" to persuade the western tribes to be vaccinated, but had failed to overcome superstition and suspicion. The epidemic of 1837 also showed that the policy of removal and isolation then under way would prove ineffective in the end. The tribes living west of the Mississippi River, farther from any white settlements than the removed eastern tribes would be, had contracted smallpox from a fur company steamboat. Civilization would not be denied.

White Efforts to Christianize Native Americans

Robert F. Berkhofer Jr.

Accompanying white traders, settlers, and soldiers were Christian missionaries intent on converting the pagan (non-Christian) Indians. Invariably, noted scholar of Indian culture Robert F. Berkhofer Jr. maintains here, these missionaries preached a mixture of religion and American cultural values. Thus, it was not simply a matter of Indians embracing Christianity while maintaining their old social and political customs; instead, religious conversion brought with it far-reaching cultural changes as the missionaries tried, in effect, to turn Indians into "white-like" Christian homesteaders. This process created deep divisions within each tribe, as some members converted, while others remained pagans (a Christian term for non-Christians). Berkhofer explains several common sequences, or scenarios, resulting from Indian Christianization, each succeeding one representing a greater division and disintegration of a tribe.

Probably the most significant turning point in the history of an Indian tribe was the loss of political autonomy. Although this point, which was usually marked by the commencement of reservation life, may have been indefinite and extended over a longer period of time in some cases than others, it was no less conclusive in each tribe. Before this point, the Indian tribal members enjoyed the traditional way of life free of outside interference and adopted the customs and artifacts of other peoples according to their own whims. Contact under these conditions has been called "non-directed" or "permissive." After the loss of political autonomy, such freedom no

Excerpted from Robert F. Berkhofer Jr., "Protestants, Pagans, and Sequences Among the North American Indians, 1760–1860," *Ethnohistory*, vol. 10, no. 3 (Summer 1963), pp. 201–216. Reprinted by permission of *Ethnohistory*. *Footnotes in the original article have been omitted in this reprint.*

longer existed, for the Indians lacked the opportunity to put space between them and the alien culture or to destroy its representatives among them without destructive reprisal. Henceforth, the members of the Indian society were under the effective control in some form of the agents of Anglo-American civilization. These representatives had an interest, and the force in the end, to alter some of the behavior and attitudes of the Indians. . . . In other words, the Americans called the tune to which the Indians danced regardless of tribal culture. This tune was composed of certain Anglo-American social and legal concepts enforced by the power of the army. . . .

Teaching Indians to Live Like Whites

Protestant missionization among the American Indians during the century between 1760 and 1860 is one confirmation of the hypothesis. An examination of the efforts of several denominations ranging from Quakers and Moravians to Baptists and Methodists as well as Presbyterians and Episcopalians among tribes as scattered as the Oneidas and Senecas of New York State, to the Cherokees and Choctaws in the South, the Ojibwa and Sioux of the Great Lakes region, and the Nez Percé of the Far West provided a good sample of white denominations as well as different tribal cultures in various stages of acculturation. In each case the story of a mission station was followed from its commencement to its extinction or survival at the end of the hundred year period. After a dozen sequences of this sort, comparison of each with the other showed certain regularities. There were four basic patterns. Before examining these sequences, we must look at the nature of missionary culture and its relation to American civilization in order to understand the determinant of the patterns.

Examination of the actual work in the field reveals few differences in aim among the missionaries of various denominations during the hundred years under study. Though many controversaries raged in the religious periodicals over the best methods of saving savages, and the century witnessed the transformation from the lonely missionary sponsored by a small society to the erection of giant manual labor boarding schools financed by prosperous national societies, all missionaries consciously and unconsciously spread much the same mixture of religion and secular pursuits. . . . For this reason the sacred and profane were combined in the minds of missionaries, and the version of their culture which they propagated may be called, as some of them termed it, "Christian Civilization." Therefore the only good Indian from their point of view was a copy of a *good* white man, or as a Methodist missionary wrote, "In school and in field, as well as in kitchen, our aim was to teach the Indians to live like white people."

The Lowliest Rung on the Ladder

That missionaries found it difficult to separate "civilization" from "Christianity" was natural, for after all they were members of their own culture and held the basic values and attitudes of that culture in common with their fellow countrymen. They dressed in contemporary style, possessed but one wife, believed in abstract justice according to the common law, ate certain foods in certain ways, and acted and thought like other Americans in most ways. At the same time missionaries represented a sub-culture within American society, for they stressed theology and moral taboos more vigorously than other citizens. Thus they adhered more strictly to the sexual code, were more honest (or were supposed to be), and were more concerned about blasphemy and obscenity than other Americans in contact with the Indians. . . . Like other whites, missionaries viewed the Indian as the lowest rung on the ladder of social evolution and believed that progress and civilization must triumph over savagery. In fact, they felt they were in the vanguard of the movement to force the aborigine up the ladder to the American apex.

Yet the missionary was only one among many whites in contact with the Indian. Soldiers, traders, and government agents usually preceded the Protestant missionary to the tribe. Although he was only one among many acculturative agents, he *demanded* more change on the part of the Indians than any other. The traders only wanted a simple bartering system implemented and perhaps a squaw. The soldiers wanted peace except when bored. The government agents desired fulfillment of treaty obligations. The blackcoat, on the other hand, sought not only religious converts but the complete transformation of Indian life. Of all the forces for acculturation between 1760 and 1860, the missionary pushed more aggressively for change than any other white, and thus provides important clues to the general understanding of Indian acculturation in this period. . . .

Christian Indians Versus Pagan Indians

When a missionary entered a new tribe, he usually settled with a local band or in a village. His efforts could not be directed at the whole tribe because of the nature of social relations in the tribe. Before white contact, a tribe was composed of small communities which managed their own affairs to a very large extent. A community was characterized by face-to-face relationships among a small group of extended families. Individual rights and obligations were determined by familial bonds in the main. Such a community was highly integrated because the people shared common values, hence goals. In itself, the societal unit, the cultural unit, and the community coincided, for the people possessing the culture were the same as those constituting the social relationships.

By the time the missionary arrived at such a village or band in the century under consideration, much acculturation had occurred, but the changes had not affected the basic social structure or cultural patterning inherited from aboriginal times. As the missionary gained converts to his program of Christian civilization, more and more Indians accepted new values and aspired to a new way of life, for just as the missionary could not really separate religion and secularism, so the Indians could not unravel the two when the blackcoat preached. For this reason, the Indians normally reacted to missionaries as to the whole of American civilization. Each culture opposed the other as a totality in this stage. Psychologically speaking there seemed to be no half-way point. Once an Indian fully surrendered to Christ, he not only observed the Sabbath and attended church, but he dressed in white man's clothing, sent his children to school, took hold of the plow, cleared his fields, began a garden, erected a house, and married his wife in a Christian ceremony—or, at least he knew he should even if he did not reach these goals. A dramatic glimpse of this feeling of totality is seen in the report of the Sioux men who dressed in white man's clothes one day to work in the fields, and the next day donned breech cloths, leggings, and blankets to conjure over the ill and attend feasts and dances. Apostasy meant putting off American-style clothing as well as Christ, even among highly acculturated Indians. Both missionaries and Indians recognized that the two cultural systems clashed, and the missionaries called the adherents of the two systems the Pagan Party and the Christian Party. We shall employ these terms for the sake of convenience to designate the native-oriented and white-oriented groups of Indians.

The success of the missionary in causing such a cultural division forced the Indians who retained the old customs to realize that they must meet the challenge to their way of life. First, the Pagan Party employed the methods of social control normally used to correct any deviation within the tribe upon those converts within the community. Social pressure ranged from mild derision to threats of personal violence against the converts. Sioux male converts, for example, were chided as being women, and the tribal "soldiers" ripped the blankets of tribesmen attending church. Some converts in this tribe were even killed. Secondly, the Pagan Party persecuted the missionary in hopes of driving him away, and in extreme cases, massacred him. At this stage of contact, the Indians frequently failed to differentiate between missionary and other American contact. . . .

The Breakdown of the Community

Somewhat more complicated is the second possible sequence which involves a social as well as cultural division. Societal disruption naturally followed from missionization, for the acceptance of new values as well as Pagan persecution demanded new social relationships. Sometimes conversion merely meant the end of polygamy. At other times couples separated because one spouse had been converted. In still other instances, people left their villages to settle in places more favorable to Indian Christianity. In extreme cases new villages or bands were formed entirely of white-oriented Indians. Thus in this sequence, after the initial cultural divisions, the cleavage worsens, and instead of reuniting as in the first sequence, the community breaks into two physically separate groups which enables each one to live in its own community in which culture and social structure coincide. . . .

[In a] third possible sequence, as more and more missionaries arrived and more whites settled around the reservation, the coincidence between culture, social structure, and community broke down not only in one village as in the preceding sequence but in many towns in the tribe. To heal the divisions, attempts were made at political organization on the tribal level. Such attempts were reinforced by the activities of government agents and missionaries. Since the Indians bordered on rapidly expanding white settlements, the governmental authorities constantly bargained for tribal lands. The peculiar ethical views of the dominant society necessitated the signing of a contract by the tribe as a whole through some legal representatives and thus fostered the notion of a more elaborate tribal government. At the same time the ever-diminishing reservation impressed the concept of territoriality, which is so essential to the modern idea of the state, upon Christian and Pagan alike. At the same time, the idea of more formal government was assisted by the missionaries who not only trained Indians in governance through church and voluntary associations organized by this time along tribal lines, but who had always strongly advocated better Indian government, that is, white law and organization. With missionary encouragement and the experience gathered in church societies, the members of the Christian Party naturally attempted to form a tribal-wide government in order to force their new culture and social relations upon their fellow tribesmen. . . .

Though the Pagans opposed the aims and even the mechanism of the Christians' political system, they would be

forced at this stage to gain power through elections and capture the new government established by the Christians. If all
had gone well, genuine political parties would have arisen.
Yet a smoothly-functioning political party system was never
realized, for neither Christians nor Pagans consented to the
other faction controlling the government in this period. The
Pagans, when they won an election, dedicated themselves to
destroying the government—or they paid no attention to
the new government at all!

Religious Divisions Lead to Political Revolution

The classic example of this sequence and its attendant troubles
is seen in Seneca history between the Revolution and the Civil
War. Until 1790 the tribe was still trying to play off British
and American officials to gain favors as had been Iroquois custom. With the decisive defeat of the Western Confederates at
Fallen Timbers, near the mouth of the Maumee River in
northwestern Ohio, and the British evacuation of the frontier
forts in 1796, they soon found themselves on reservations
formed around their villages in scattered locations in western
New York State. As soon as all had quieted, the Philadelphia
Friends, who had become interested in the Seneca chief Corn-
planter during his visits to the young United States Capital,
established a mission on his reservation. . . .

Community divisions were prevalent on the four major re-
serves by the eve of the War of 1812. The full development
of a tribal-wide split along Pagan and Christian lines is
marked by a council in 1819, which was called to consider
other questions but actually debated whether the Senecas
should adopt white customs and institutions. This intra-tribal
bickering was exacerbated by the Ogden Land Company's attempt to purchase the Seneca reservations in the 1820's and
the Federal Government's efforts to remove the tribe in the
following decade, which culminated in the Buffalo Creek
Treaty of 1838. Many members claimed this treaty, by which
the tribe ceded all their lands, was fraudulent, and they and
the Quakers obtained its repudiation after a four year struggle. Dissatisfaction with the chiefs' role in this affair brought
forth experiments in tribal government. . . .

Which provided for a government of three branches: a legislature composed of 18 members elected annually, an executive, and a judiciary of three peacemakers for each reservation. Other tribal officers elected annually by all males over 21 were the clerk, treasurer, superintendent of schools, overseers of the poor, assessors, and overseers of the highway as well as a marshal and two deputies for each reserve. This revolution was no more successful (although less bloody) than its more important counterparts overseas, for the "Old Chiefs' Party" fought this government till the end of the period under discussion and secured modifications.

Mixing Religion and Politics

Certainly it is evident, even in this brief analysis, that the missionaries were only a partial cause of the Seneca Revolution and that governmental pressures and other acculturative forces played a large part. After 1819, the difference between Pagan and Christian no longer revolved about the acceptance of white ways so much as the speed and degree of adoption. Some of the Pagan Party, in fact, allied themselves with the Quakers in the 1820's after the Christian Party had turned to the Presbyterians. . . . The Indian culture and social relations had become so fragmented under white contact that the natives could perceive the subtle differences in the views and behavior of the whites and classify them accordingly.

This points up the last possible sequence of missionization. Given conditions of advanced acculturation and tribal division, missionaries entering a tribe then were thrown into an already existing faction rather than aiding in the creation of one. Such a possibility is seen in Cherokee and Choctaw history, where missionaries were automatically involved in factional politics revolving about removal and later slavery, in spite of their efforts at dissociation. Under these circumstances, Indian church members switched religious affiliation according to politics. For instance, a leading Choctaw left the church of a Presbyterian missionary from the North and organized a Cumberland Presbyterian Church which was more in line with his sentiments toward the Negro. In other words, the Indians had acculturated to the point where they could not only differentiate the various elements of American civilization, but were themselves divided according to their perceptions of the various elements.

Although this last sequence points to the eventual and complete assimilation of the Indian, such was not to happen after the Civil War. Instead, greater fragmentation followed acculturation, and Americans always have refused final acceptance of the Indian because of racial prejudice. Furthermore, as the government took over work in the field, the missionary became less significant as the major acculturative force. We should remember, of course, that the missionary had only spearheaded acculturation in the absence of government activity during the century under study and was always within its control. Yet, when the missionary was the chief force, he and the response to him provide many clues to the nature of cultural change.

Chapter 4

Epilogue: Legacy of the Indian Wars

Turning|Points
IN WORLD HISTORY

Assimilation Versus Self-Determination: American Indians in the Twentieth Century

Carl Waldman

In a very real sense, Native American battles for survival, fair treatment, and respect did not end with the close of the Indian wars in the 1890s. As Carl Waldman, formerly of the New York State Historical Association, tells it here, all through the twentieth century, Indians had to deal with frequently shifting U.S. government policies that often ignored their best interests, held them back economically and socially, and sought to trivialize or eradicate traditional tribal customs. One popular approach (at least among whites) was assimilation (or acculturation), the attempt to absorb Indian peoples and their cultures into the American mainstream. The policy operated on the assumption that Indians were better off acting and thinking like whites. Eventually, a combination of changing white attitudes and the efforts of Indian activists demanding better treatment for their peoples brought a new approach. From the 1970s to the present, Indian life and affairs have been characterized more by self-determination; driven by the goal of restoring tribal ways, integrity, and self-sufficiency; and based on the assumption that Indian culture enriches both Indians and whites and should be treasured.

The subject matter of Indian studies is not remote and fixed in time but, rather, relevant and current. As those people living near reservations or other Indian communities realize, as do those interested in Indian art or minority sociology and politics, there is a sizable and vital Native North American population with contemporary concerns and aspirations. The Indian story of course did not end in the 19th century, after the Wars for the West, but continues right up to the present. . . .

Some of the relevant and often contradictory concepts [and issues affecting American Indians in the twentieth century include] . . . tribal sovereignty, treaties, federal trust responsibility, federal bureaucracy, Indian removal and concentration, boundaries and reservations, assimilation, and land allotment. . . .

Attempts to Assimilate and "Civilize" Indians

The white policy toward Indians of assimilation was not new. Missionaries and educators had been practicing it since the earliest colonial times, striving to Christianize and "civilize" Indians, assuming they were bestowing upon them a better life. During the late 19th century, after the period of separation as governmental policy, in which the primary objective was the removal of Indians from lands desired by whites, acculturation under duress, detribalization, and Americanization followed. The stated official goal was the self-sufficiency of Indian peoples, but it was self-sufficiency through terms dictated by whites—i.e., the suppression of Indian culture and the adoption by Indians of white traditions and technologies. The means to the end became allotment.

In 1887, the United States Congress passed the General Allotment Act (or the Dawes Severalty Act), under which Indian reservations were to be broken up and allotted to the heads of Indian families in 160-acre pieces, with the rationale that the lands would then be developed and farmed by economically motivated landholders. After the assignment of plots to Indians, any surplus territory would be distributed to non-Indians with the idea of bringing about the maximum utilization of tillable lands. In 1891, because of the continuing disuse of many of the parcels by Indians, followup legislation provided for the leasing of their allotted lands to whites. And when the Cherokees and Choctaws of the Indian Territory refused allotment, taking their case to federal courts, Congress passed the Curtis Act of 1898, which dissolved their tribal governments and extended land allotment policy to them. . . .

Thus, coming into the 20th century, Indians were subject to a federal policy that sought to eliminate tribal landholdings and political organizations, suppress communal customs, and terminate trust status. At the end of the trust period, when so-called Indian "competency" was established—a 25-year schedule had originally been projected in 1887—Indians were to be granted citizenship. . . .

In 1924, after the projected 25-year period but before the large majority of Indians had proven "competency," Congress passed the Citizenship Act, granting all Indians citizenship (although some states still withheld the right to vote; New Mexico, Arizona, and Maine did not grant it until after World War II). The impetus for citizenship resulted in part from the Indian contribution in World War I. But an additional motive was the hope for more rapid assimilation.

Caught Between Two Worlds

Yet, by the 1920s, the concepts of both assimilation and allotment were being widely questioned. Coercive acculturation had created a cultureless generation, caught between two worlds. Tribal governments had been replaced by a paternalistic and unresponsive federal bureaucracy. And many Indians in the allotted tribes had lost not only their cultural and tribal identity but also their potential economic base— their land. During the entire period of allotment, Indians were dispossessed of millions of acres, nearly two-thirds of the total held in 1887. . . .

In 1934, under socially progressive President Franklin D. Roosevelt and his commissioner of Indian Affairs, John Collier, who had founded the American Indian Defense Association, Congress passed the Indian Reorganization Act (or the Wheeler-Howard Act). Reversing the policies of assimilation and allotment, this act gave legal sanction to tribal landholdings; resumed unsold allotted lands to tribes; made provisions for the purchase of new lands; encouraged tribal constitutions, systems of justice, and business corporations; expanded educational opportunities through new facilities and loans, with an emphasis on reservation day schools instead of off-reservation boarding schools; advocated the hiring of Indians by the Bureau of Indian Affairs and Indian involvement in management and policy making at national and tribal levels; extended the Indian trust status; and granted Indians religious freedom. . . .

During the 1950s, the federal government would reverse its approach to Indians once again with a renewed coercive assimilationist policy.

Voluntary Relocation?

Proponents of the termination of the federal-Indian trust relationship and Indian assimilation into the cultural mainstream, notably commissioners of Indian Affairs Dillon Myer and Glenn Emmons plus Senator Arthur Watkins of Utah, came to shape the United States Indian policies of the 1950s and early 1960s. To achieve Indian acculturation, they also advocated the relocation of Indians to urban centers. The report of the Hoover Commission on the Reorganization of Government in 1949, recommending termination, became the basis for the series of governmental resolutions.

In 1952, Congress established a Voluntary Relocation Program, which offered counseling and guidance before relocation as well as assistance in finding residence and employment in the new community. In 1953, Congress passed the Termination Resolution (House Concurrent Resolution 108), which called for Indian equality under the law as well as the release of certain tribes from federal supervision. That same year, Public Law 280 gave certain states civil and criminal jurisdiction over Indian reservations without the consent of tribes. . . .

Meanwhile, from 1954 to 1962, Congress terminated the federal relationship with 61 tribes, bands, and communities. Among the largest were the Menominees of Wisconsin. Although termination was presented to them as freedom from further federal intervention, an underlying motive for various private white interests and their allies in Congress centered around the acquisition of timber on Indian lands. After termination, the new Menominee corporation, Menominee

Enterprises, Inc., encountered economic setbacks in the lumber business. Many tribal members lost their lands because of an inability to pay the new property taxes. And without federally sponsored social, educational, and health services and facilities, the tribe sunk deeper and deeper into poverty. As a result, a coalition of Menominee factions along with non-Indian supporters lobbied for restoration of trust status for the tribe and reservation status for remaining lands. In 1974, Congress finally complied, passing the Menominee Restoration Act. Four years later, Congress also restored the federal government's trust relationship with the Ottawas, Wyandots, Peorias, and Modocs. . . .

Tribal Restoration and Self-Sufficiency

Termination as official federal policy came to an end during the 1960s, although various programs from the termination period carried over even to the 1970s. The catchall phrase used to describe United States Indian policy from the 1960s to the present is "Indian Self-Determination," which embraces a variety of concepts, including tribal restoration, self-government, cultural renewal, development of reservation resources, and self-sufficiency, as well as the ongoing special Indian and federal trust relationship for the protection of the trust assets and the provision of economic and social programs needed to raise the standard of living of Indian peoples to a level comparable to the rest of society. The thrust of the policy of course has varied with changing federal administrations. And Indian leaders themselves have advocated varying aspects of it, as consistent with the meaning of the phrase itself, which expresses Indian involvement and choice.

A number of governmental studies and commissions were pivotal in the trend away from termination and towards self-determination: In 1961, three commissions—the Keeler Commission on Indian Affairs; the Brophy Commission on Rights, Liberties, and Responsibilities of the American Indian; and the United States Commission on Civil Rights—recommended more constructive Indian programs supporting Indian self-determination and fostering Indian economic and social equality. . . .

In 1977, the American Indian Policy Review Commission opposed forced assimilation of Indian peoples and advocated tribal self-determination and self-government.

The Birth of Indian Activism

Just as these various studies and commissions increased society's awareness of the Indian condition, so did the work of Indian activists who, in a mood of growing militancy, founded many new pan-Indian groups and staged many political events and demonstrations. . . .

Throughout the years preceding World War II and through the 1940s and 1950s, Indian activism was nonviolent, with an emphasis on legal remedies. In 1922, as a symbolic gesture, Deskaheh, a Cayuga chief, traveled to the League of Nations in Geneva, Switzerland, to obtain recognition of his tribe's sovereignty, which was denied. Again symbolically, in 1939, the Seneca Nation at Tonawanda issued a "Declaration of Independence" to the state of New York. During World War II, whereas many Indians fought and died for the United States, and the Iroquois League even went so far as to independently declare war on Germany, others resisted selective service laws and were jailed, among them Iroquois, Utes, Papagos, Hopis, and Seminoles.

After the war, many tribes and organizations resisted the new federal termination policy. DRUMS, or Determination of Rights and Unity for Menominee Shareholders, helped bring about restoration of the tribe's trust status. During this period, many tribes also offered resistance to various reclamation projects forced on them by the governmental concept of eminent domain. For example, the Senecas sought legal grounds to prevent the building of Kinzua Dam in Pennsylvania (1958); the Tuscaroras resisted the Tuscarora Power Project of the New York State Power Authority (1957–58); and the Miccosukees fought the Everglades Reclamation Project in Florida (1958). . . .

A Struggle for "Red Power"

In the 1960s and 1970s, however, Native American resistance took on a new dimension. Many of the new activist leaders were college-educated and radicalized youth influenced by the civil rights and counterculture movements in other segments of society. Many also lived in urban areas, their parents having resettled there as a result of federal relocation programs. Many were at odds with the generally older, more politically conservative tribal leaders, some of whom they believed to be, in effect, dupes of an interventionist, colonialist government and exploitative corporate interests. As far as the new activists were concerned, not only had the federal government failed to fulfill the promises of its treaties, acts, and agreements in correcting the miserable Indian socioeconomic conditions, but federal officials continued to act bureaucratically and presumptively in Indian affairs, as if they alone knew what was best for Indian peoples. Activists were also concerned with continuing racial discrimination in housing and employment, as well as police brutality against Indians. The only hope for true social reform, they believed, was not surrogate action by whites but direct Native American political action, including wide-based pan-Indian organization and lobbying, plus occasional demonstrations, vandalism, and acts of violence to draw public attention to the Indian plight from an otherwise somnolent, uncaring society.

The history of the Indian movement since the 1960s—the struggle for "Red Power"—involves many incidents, individuals, organizations, and publications on both the tribal and national level. . . .

The most important organization, in terms of recent activism, turned out to be the American Indian Movement (AIM), founded in Minneapolis in 1968 by the Chippewas Dennis Banks, George Mitchell, and Clyde Bellecourt, as well as the Sioux Russell Means, who became spokesmen for urban Indians. AIM more than any other group was responsible for the upsurge in militant political action in the late 1960s and early 1970s, especially the occupation of federally held property to dramatize the Native American cause. The takeover of the abandoned island of Alcatraz in 1969 gained worldwide attention and support. But when public interest waned by 1971, federal marshals made their move and dislodged the dissidents. In less-publicized events, Indian activists occupied the federal building in Littleton, Colorado; Ft. Lawton in Washington; Mt. Rushmore; Stanley Island; Ellis Island; and the Coast Guard Station on Lake Michigan. Another dramatic action of the period was the Trail of Broken Treaties Caravan in 1972, consisting of a march on Washington, D.C., and the subsequent six-day demonstration during which dissidents occupied Bureau of Indian Affairs (BIA) offices and destroyed public files.

Then, the following year, 1973, AIM members and supporters occupied the Sioux Pine Ridge reservation in South Dakota, the site of the Wounded Knee Massacre of 1890. The occupation grew out of a dispute among the Indians themselves. Young activists demonstrated against what they considered to be the autocratic and sometimes corrupt practices of the elder Sioux leaders. But the occupation evolved into a state of siege, with the dissidents holding out behind roadblocks and barriers against federal agents. One of the Indian demands was a review of the historical treaties, between the federal government and the tribes, that AIM alleged had been broken. By the time a settlement had been reached, after 71 days of alternate shootings, negotiations, and inactivity, two Indians, Frank Clearwater and Buddy Lamont, had been killed and a federal marshal wounded. AIM leaders were subsequently indicted, but the case was dismissed on grounds of misconduct by the prosecution.

A second shootout on the Pine Ridge reservation in 1975 led to the death of two FBI agents and the conviction of Leonard Peltier, . . . whose situation [became] a rallying point for Indian activists. . . .

A Newfound Indian Identity

Another positive development since the days of coercive assimilation earlier in the century is tribal restoration. Cohesive in nature, tribes serve as large extended families for members. Although reservations often reveal a shocking degree of poverty, they all manifest a degree of social integration and community rarely found in other parts of American and Canadian society. Moreover, tribes function as business concerns or corporations, protecting and serving individual interests. There is widespread Indian participation at the tribal level, more than found at most other local levels of society. Tribes have increasingly taken control of their destiny from the federal bureaucracy and, when possible, from outside exploitative interests. And there are tribal economic success stories—solid incomes or, in some instances, even fortunes made through tourism, industrial development, and wise investment of land-claim awards.

Along with tribal restoration comes newfound Indian identity. A growing number of pan-Indian coalitions, organizations, publications, and powwows have contributed to this sense of common purpose, even at the international level. Differences between various factions—one tribe and others; reservation Indians and urban Indians; elders and youth; assimilationists and traditionalists; conservatives and activists; whatever the breakdown—increasingly have been resolved since the political catharsis of the 1960s and 1970s, and common threats to Indian progress have been recognized. Practically all the tribes and factions have grown in political and legal awareness. Indians are less likely than ever to be exploited by bureaucrats and businessmen. Religion plays a large part in this pan-Indian revitalization, organizations such as the Native American Church having a large intertribal membership. The Indian Religion Freedom Act of 1978 has given Indian groups new legal ammunition in the protection of sacred lands.

Self-betterment for some Indians has meant integration into the American mainstream. Educated and trained individuals are found in fields other than the arts—civil service, academia, medicine, law—as well as in blue-collar professions, such as high-steel construction. Some stay in close cultural contact with other Indians, choosing to live or work among them. For those who do not, their "Indianness" fosters a greater sense of pride than ever before in this century. And whites now often brag about any Indian ancestry they have. . . .

A National Treasure

There is another aspect to the Indian contribution that is more difficult to measure and that can be called the philo-

sophical or the spiritual element in the Indian example. Indians represent heroic and romantic historical figures who
held out, through skill and courage, against overwhelming
forces. They also represent beings who were in tune with
themselves, one another, and nature. Balance and harmony
are concepts often applied to Indian ways of life, as well as to
Indian inner life. For societies alarmed by ecological damage
from modern technologies, Indian coexistence with the natural environment serves as a model for survival. And Indian
humor, stoicism, and focus serve as inspiration. The Indian
world view continues to have relevance.

For civilizations based on cultural pluralism, native peoples should hold symbolic places of honor as the first North
Americans. And, for having been deprived of most of what
was once all their land by the people who came after them,
they should be granted the necessary means to achieve their
social and cultural goals. Native North American culture in
both the United States and Canada is a national treasure. Its
renewal is everyone's renewal.

Appendix

Excerpts from Original Documents Pertaining to the North American Indian Wars

Differing Visions of the World and Each Other

Document 1: Indians Are "Savages" and "Murderers"

The prevailing white view of most Indians during the period in which the United States was gaining its independence from Britain was summed up by a Pittsburgh resident, Hugh Brackenridge, in this letter written in the early 1780s to the editor of the then widely read Freeman's Journal.

Having an opportunity to know something of the character of this race of men [the Indians], from the deeds they perpetrate daily round me, I think it proper to say something on the subject. Indeed, several years ago, and before I left your city, I had thought different from some others with respect to the right of soil, and the propriety of forming treaties and making peace with them.

In the United States Magazine in the year 1777, I published a dissertation denying them to have a right in the soil. I perceive a writer in your very elegant and useful paper, has taken up the same subject, under the signature of "Caractacus," and unanswerably shown, that their claim to the extensive countries of America, is wild and inadmissible. I will take the liberty in this place, to pursue this subject a little.

On what is their claim founded?—Occupancy. A wild Indian with his skin painted red, and a feather through his nose, has set his foot on the broad continent of North and South America; a second wild Indian with his ears cut in ringlets, or his nose slit like a swine or a malefactor, also sets his foot on the same extensive tract of soil. Let the first Indian make a talk to his brother, and bid him take his foot off the continent, for he being first upon it, had occupied the whole, to kill buffaloes, and tall elks with long horns. This claim in the reasoning of some men would be just, and the second savage ought to depart in his canoe, and seek a continent where no prior occupant claimed the soil. . . .

The whole of this earth was given to man, and all descendants of Adam have a right to share it equally. There is no right of primogeniture in the laws of nature and of nations. There is reason that a tall man, such as the chaplain in the American army we call the High Priest, should have a large spot of ground to stretch himself upon; or that a man with a big belly, like a goodly alderman of London, should have a larger garden to produce beans and cabbage for his appetite, but that an agile, nimble runner, like an Indian called the Big Cat, at Fort Pitt, should have more than his neighbors, because he has traveled a great space, I can see no reason. . . .

It is said that an individual, building a house or fabricating a machine, has an exclusive right to it, and why not those who improve the earth? I would say, should man build houses on a greater part of the soil, than falls to his share, I would, in a state of nature, take away a proportion of the soil and the houses from him, but a machine or any work of art, does not lessen the means of subsistence to the human race, which an extensive occupation of the soil does.

Claims founded on the first discovery of soil are futile. When gold, jewels, manufactures, or any work of men's hands is lost, the finder is entitled to some reward, that is, he has some claims on the thing found, for a share of it. . . .

With regard to forming treaties or making peace with this race, there are many ideas:

They have the shapes of men and may be of the human species, but certainly in their present state they approach nearer the character of Devils; take an Indian, is there any faith in him? Can you bind him by favors? Can you trust his word or confide in his promise? When he makes war upon you, when he takes you prisoner and has you in his power, will he spare you? In this he departs from the law of nature. . . . On this principle are not the whole Indian nations murderers?

Many of them may have not had an opportunity of putting prisoners to death, but the sentiment which they entertain leads them invariably to this when they have it in their power or judge it expedient; these principles constitute them murderers, and they ought to be prevented from carrying them into execution, as we would prevent a common homicide, who should be mad enough to conceive himself justifiable in killing men. . . .

If we could have any faith in the promises they make we could suffer them to live, provided they would only make war amongst themselves, and abandon their hiding or lurking on the pathways of our citizens, emigrating unarmed and defenceless inhabitants;

and murdering men, women and children in a defenceless situation; and on their ceasing in the meantime to raise arms no more among the American Citizens.

Quoted in Wilcomb E. Washburn, ed., *The Indian and the White Man*. Garden City, NY: Doubleday, 1964, pp. 111–17.

Document 2: Whites Are "Ungrateful" and "Unjust"

Having been exploited by the French, British, and others in colonial days, at the time the United States was coming into being most Indians who had had dealings with whites expressed negative feelings about them. In this example, a white clergyman, John Heckewelder, quotes Mohican spokesmen of the 1760s and 1770s.

Long and dismal are the complaints which the Indians make of European ingratitude and injustice. Often I have listened to these descriptions of their hard sufferings until I felt ashamed of being a white man. . . .

They begin with the Virginians, whom they call the long knives. . . . "It was we," say the Lenape, Mohicans, and their kindred tribes, "who so kindly received them on their first arrival into our country. We took them by the hand, and bid them welcome to sit down by our side, and live with us as brothers; but how did they requite our kindness? They at first asked only for a little land on which to raise bread for themselves and their families, and pasture for their cattle, which we freely gave them. They soon wanted more, which we also gave them. They saw the game in the woods, which the Great Spirit had given us for our subsistence, and they wanted that too. They penetrated into the woods in quest of game; they discovered spots of land which pleased them; that land they also wanted, and because we were loth to part with it, as we saw they had already more than they had need of, they took it from us by force, and drove us to a great distance from our ancient homes."

Quoted in Wilbur R. Jacobs, *Dispossessing the American Indian: Indians and Whites on the Colonial Frontier*. New York: Scribner's, 1972, p. 59.

Document 3: Indian Versus White Civility

Benjamin Franklin, one of the fairest and most perceptive of the U.S. founders, saw much to be admired about American Indians, as evidenced by this 1784 comparison of white and Indian manners. It should be noted, however, that, despite his many positive remarks about Indians, Franklin still refers to them as "savages."

Savages we call them, because their manners differ from ours, which we think the perfection of civility; they think the same of theirs.

Perhaps, if we could examine the manners of different nations with impartiality, we should find no people so rude, as to be without any rules of politeness; nor any so polite, as not to have some remains of rudeness.

The Indian men, when young, are hunters and warriors; when old, counsellors; for all their government is by counsel of the sages; there is no force, there are no prisons, no officers to compel obedience, or inflict punishment. Hence they generally study oratory, the best speaker having the most influence. The Indian women till the ground, dress the food, nurse and bring up the children, and preserve and hand down to posterity the memory of public transactions. These employments of men and women are accounted natural and honorable. Having few artificial wants, they have abundance of leisure for improvement by conversation. Our laborious manner of life, compared with theirs, they esteem slavish and base; and the learning on which we value ourselves they regard as frivolous and useless. An instance of this occurred at the Treaty of Lancaster, in Pennsylvania, *anno* 1744, between the Government of Virginia and the Six Nations. After the principal business was settled, the commissioners from Virginia acquainted the Indians by a speech that there was at Williamsburg a College, with a fund for educating Indian youth; and that if the Six Nations would send down half a dozen of their young lads to that college, the government would take care that they should be well provided for and instructed in all the learning of the white people. It is one of the Indian rules of politeness not to answer a public proposition the same day that it is made; they think it would be treating it as a light matter and that they show it respect by taking time to consider it, as a matter important. They therefore deferred their answer till the day following; when their speaker began by expressing their deep sense of the kindness of the Virginia government in making them that offer; "for we know," says he, "that you highly esteem the kind of learning taught in those colleges, and that the maintenance of our young men, while with you, would be very expensive to you. We are convinced, therefore, that you mean to do us good by your proposal; and we thank you heartily. But you, who are wise, must know that different nations have different conceptions of things; and you will therefore not take it amiss, if our ideas of this kind of education happen not to be the same with yours. We have had some experience of it; several of our young people were formerly brought up at the colleges of the northern provinces; they were instructed in all your sciences; but, when they came back to us, they were bad runners, ignorant of every means of living in the woods, unable to bear either cold or hunger, knew neither how to build a cabin, take a deer, or kill an enemy, spoke our language imperfectly, were therefore neither fit for hunters, warriors, nor counsellors; they were totally good for nothing. We are however not the less obliged by your kind offer, though we decline accepting it; and, to show our grateful sense of it, if the gentlemen of Virginia will send us a dozen of their sons, we will take great care of their education, instruct them in all we know, and make *Men* of them.". . .

The politeness of these savages in conversation is indeed carried to excess, since it does not permit them to contradict or deny the truth of what is asserted in their presence. By this means they indeed avoid disputes; but then it becomes difficult to know their minds, or what impression you make upon them. The missionaries who have attempted to convert them to Christianity, all complain of this as one of the great difficulties of their mission. The Indians hear with patience the truths of the gospel explained to them, and give their usual tokens of assent and approbation; you would think they were convinced. No such matter. It is mere civility.

A Swedish minister, having assembled the chiefs of the Susquehanah Indians, made a sermon to them, acquainting them with the principal historical facts on which our religion is founded; such as the fall of our first parents by eating an apple, the coming of Christ to repair the mischief, his miracles and suffering, etc. When he had finished, an Indian orator stood up to thank him. "What you have told us," says he, "is all very good. It is indeed bad to eat apples. It is better to make them all into cider. We are much obliged by your kindness in coming so far, to tell us these things which you have heard from your mothers. In return, I will tell you some of those we have heard from ours. In the beginning, our fathers had only the flesh of animals to subsist on; and if their hunting was unsuccessful, they were starving. Two of our young hunters, having killed a deer, made a fire in the woods to broil some part of it. When they were about to satisfy their hunger, they beheld a beautiful young woman descend from the clouds, and seat herself on that hill, which you see yonder among the blue mountains. They said to each other, it is a spirit that has smelt our broiling venison, and wishes to eat of it; let us offer some to her. They presented her with the tongue; she was pleased with the taste of it, and said, 'Your kindness shall be rewarded; come to this place after thirteen moons, and you shall find something that will be of great benefit in nourishing you and your children to the latest generations.' They did so, and, to their surprise, found plants they had never seen before; but which, from that ancient time, have been constantly cultivated among us, to our great advantage. Where her right hand had touched the ground, they found maize; where her left hand had touched it, they found kidney-beans; and where her backside had sat on it, they found tobacco." The good missionary, disgusted with this idle tale, said, "What I delivered to you were sacred truths; but what you tell me is mere fable, fiction, and falsehood." The Indian, offended, replied, "My brother, it seems your friends have not done you justice in your education; they have not well instructed you in the rules of common civility. You saw that we, who understand and practice those rules, believed all your stories; why do you refuse to believe ours?"

When any of them come into our towns, our people are apt to crowd round them, gaze upon them, and incommode them, where they desire to be private; this they esteem great rudeness, and the effect of the want of instruction in the rules of civility and good manners. "We have," say they, "as much curiosity as you, and when you come into our towns, we wish for opportunities of looking at you; but for this purpose we hide ourselves behind bushes, where you are to pass, and never intrude ourselves into your company."

Their manner of entering one another's village has likewise its rules. It is reckoned uncivil in travelling strangers to enter a village abruptly, without giving notice of their approach. Therefore, as soon as they arrive within hearing, they stop and hollow, remaining there till invited to enter. Two old men usually come out to them, and lead them in. There is in every village a vacant dwelling, called *the Strangers' House*. Here they are placed, while the old men go round from hut to hut, acquainting the inhabitants, that strangers are arrived, who are probably hungry and weary; and every one sends them what he can spare of victuals, and skins to repose on. When the strangers are refreshed, pipes and tobacco are brought; and then, but not before, conversation begins, with inquiries who they are, whither bound, what news, etc.; and it usually ends with offers of service, if the strangers have occasion of guides, or any necessaries for continuing their journey; and nothing is exacted for the entertainment.

Remarks Concerning the Savages of North America, 1784, quoted in Nancy B. Black and Bette S. Weidman, eds., *White on Red: Images of the American Indian*. Port Washington, NY: Kennikat Press, 1976, pp. 102–105.

Document 4: Indians Compared with Early Europeans

In this 1781 tract, renowned U.S. founder Thomas Jefferson questions the validity of the theory, then widely accepted by educated whites, that animals and people originating in the Americas are naturally inferior to those bred in Europe.

Before we condemn the Indians of this continent as wanting genius, we must consider that letters have not yet been introduced among them. Were we to compare them in their present state with the Europeans north of the Alps, when the Roman arms and arts first crossed those mountains, the comparison would be unequal, because, at that time, those parts of Europe were swarming with numbers; because numbers produce emulation, and multiply the chances of improvement, and one improvement begets another. Yet I may safely ask, How many good poets, how many able mathematicians, how many great inventors in arts or sciences, had Europe north of the Alps then produced? And it was sixteen centuries after this before a Newton could be formed. I do not mean to deny, that there are varieties in the race of man, distinguished by their powers both of body and mind. I believe there are, as I see to be the case in the races of other animals. I only mean to suggest a doubt, whether the bulk and faculties of animals depend on the side of the Atlantic on which their food happens to grow, or which furnishes the elements of which they are compounded? Whether nature has enlisted herself as a . . . Trans-Atlantic partisan? I am induced to suspect, there has been more eloquence than sound reasoning displayed in support of this theory; that it is one of those cases where the judgment has been seduced by a glowing pen: and whilst I render every tribute of honor and esteem to the celebrated zoologist, who has added, and is still adding, so many precious things to the treasures of science, I must doubt whether in this instance he has not cherished error also, by lending her for a moment his vivid imagination and bewitching language.

Notes on the State of Virginia, ed. William Peden. Chapel Hill: University of North Carolina Press, 1955, p. 64.

Document 5: Savagery Must Give Way to Civilization

In an 1833 statement that lent support to what would later come to be called manifest destiny, the white belief that Providence had ordained the U.S. to enjoy unlimited expansion, Massachusetts missionary Timothy Flint argues that the march of white civilization over the lands of Indian "savages" conforms to the laws of nature.

In the whole history of the incipient settlement of our country, not one solitary instance of an attempt to settle an unoccupied tract, claimed by the natives, is to be found, which was not succeeded by all the revolting details of Indian warfare. It is of little importance to enquire, which party was the aggressor. The natives were not sufficient civilians to distinguish between the right of empire and the right of soil. Beside a repulsion of nature, an incomparability of character and pursuit, they constantly saw in every settler a new element to effect their expulsion from their native soil. Our industry, fixed residences, modes, laws, institutions, schools, religion, rendered an union with them as incompatible as with animals of another nature. . . . In the unchangeable order of things, two such races can not exist together, each preserving its co-ordinate identity. Either this great continent, in the order of Providence, should have remained in the occupancy of half a million of savages, engaged in everlasting conflicts of their peculiar warfare with each other, or it must have become, as it has, the domain of civilized millions. It is in vain to charge upon the latter race results, which grew out of the laws of nature, and the universal march of human events. Let the same occupancy of the American wilderness by the municipal European be repeated, if it could be, under the control of the most philanthropic eulogists of the savages, and every reasoning mind will discover, that in the gradual ascendancy of the one race, the decline of the other must have been a consequence, and that substantially the same annals would be repeated, as the dark and revolting incidents which we have to record. We do not say, that the aggression has not been in innumerable instances on the part of the whites. We do not deny, that the white borderers have too often been more savage, than the Indians themselves. . . . But still in the Indian animal and moral structure, their ancient propensities would be found, we doubt not, as vigorous as ever among those remnants the most subdued and modified by our institutions. Give them scope, development, and an object, place them in view of an equal or inferior enemy, and their instinctive nature would again raise the war-whoop, and wield the scalping knife, and renew the Indian warfare of the bygone days.

Indian Wars of the West; Containing Biographical Sketches of Those Pioneers Who Headed the Western Settlers in Repelling the Attacks of the Savages, quoted in Wilcomb E. Washburn, ed., *The Indian and the White Man.* Garden City, NY: Doubleday, 1964, pp. 125–27.

Document 6: A Kinship with the Earth

This statement expressing the Indians' "oneness," so to speak, with the environment is by Chief Luther Standing Bear (born 1868), a Lakota (western Sioux). The chief's sentiment contrasts sharply with the conception of his white contemporaries, namely that of the earth and environment as commodities to be exploited.

The Lakota was a true naturist—a lover of nature. He loved the earth and all things of the earth, the attachment growing with age. The old people came literally to love the soil and they sat or reclined on the ground with a feeling of being close to a mothering power. It was good for the skin to touch the earth and the old people liked to remove their moccasins and walk with bare feet on the sacred earth. Their tipis were built upon the earth and their altars were made of earth. The birds that flew in the air came to rest upon the earth and it was the final abiding place of all things that lived and grew. The soil was soothing, strengthening, cleansing and healing.

That is why the old Indian still sits upon the earth instead of propping himself up and away from its life-giving forces. For him, to sit or lie upon the ground is to be able to think more deeply and to feel more keenly; he can see more clearly into the mysteries of life and come closer in kinship to other lives about him. . . .

Kinship with all creatures of the earth, sky and water was a real and active principle. For the animal and bird world there existed a brotherly feeling that kept the Lakota safe among them and so close did some of the Lakotas come to their feathered and furred friends that in true brotherhood they spoke a common tongue.

The old Lakota was wise. He knew that man's heart away from nature becomes hard; he knew that lack of respect for growing, living things soon led to lack of respect for humans too. So he kept his youth close to its softening influence.

Quoted in T.C. McLuhan, *Touch the Earth: A Self-Portrait of Indian Existence.* New York: Promontory Press, 1971, p. 6.

Document 7: Indians and Whites Incompatible?

In 1822, Petalesharo, a Pawnee chief, gave the following answer to President James Monroe, who had invited him to sign a friendship pact with the United States. The chief's eloquent statement suggests that, while it is desirable for the white and red races to coexist in peace, their ways and views may be too different to cultivate true friendship.

My Great Father . . . The Great Spirit made us all—he made my skin red, and yours white, he placed us on this earth, and intended that we should live differently from each other.

He made the whites to cultivate the earth, and feed on domestic animals, but he made us, redskins, to rove through the uncultivated woods and plains, to feed on wild animals, and to dress with their skins. He also intended that we should go to war, to take scalps, steal horses from and triumph over our enemies, cultivate peace at home, and promote the happiness of each other. I believe there are no people of my color on this earth who do not believe in the Great Spirit—in rewards and punishments. We worship him, but we worship him not as you do. We differ from you in appearance and manners as well as in our customs, and we differ from you in our religion; we have no large houses as you have to worship the Great Spirit in; if we had them today, we would want others tomorrow, for we have not, like you, a fixed habitation—we have no settled home except our villages, where we remain but two moons in twelve. We, like animals, rove through the country, whilst you whites reside between us and heaven; but still, my Great Father, we love the Great Spirit—we acknowledge his supreme power—our peace, our health, and our happiness depend upon him, and our lives belong to him—he made us and he can destroy us.

My Great Father. Some of your good chiefs [missionaries], as they are called, have proposed to send some of their good people among us to change our habits, to make us work and live like the white people. I will not tell a lie—I am going to tell the truth. You love your country, you love your people, you love the manner in which they live, and you think your people brave. I am like you, my Great Father, I love my country, I love my people, I love the manner in which they live, and think myself and warriors brave. Spare me then, Father, let me enjoy my country, and pursue the buffalo, and the beaver, and the other wild animals of our country, and I will trade their skins with your people. I have grown up and lived thus long without work—I am in hopes you will suffer me to die without it. We have plenty of buffalo, deer, and other wild animals—we have also an abundance of horses. We have everything we want, we have plenty of land, if you will keep your people off of it. . . .

It is too soon, my Great Father, to send those good men among us. We are not starving yet—we wish you to permit us to enjoy the chase until the game of our country is exhausted, until the wild animals have become extinct. Let us exhaust our present resources before you make us toil and interrupt our happiness—let me continue to live as I have done, and after I have passed to the good or evil spirit from off the wilderness of my present life, the subsistence of my children may become so precarious as to need and embrace the assistance of those good people.

Quoted in Annette Rosenstiel, *Red and White: Indian Views of the White Man, 1492–1982.* New York: Universe Books, 1983, pp. 116–17.

Document 8: "There Is But One Religion"

This powerfully worded 1805 exchange between Red Jacket, a Seneca chief, and a Boston missionary effectively captures the huge religious and cultural rift separating the red and white races during the United States' first century.

Missionary:

"*My Friends;* I am thankful for the opportunity afforded us of uniting together at this time. I had a great desire to see you, and inquire into your state and welfare; for this purpose I have travelled a great distance, being sent by your old friends, the Boston Missionary Society. You will recollect they formerly sent missionaries among you, to instruct you in religion, and labor for your good. Although they have not heard from you for a long time, yet they have not forgotten their brothers the Six Nations, and are still anxious to do you good.

"*Brothers;* I have not come to get your lands or your money, but to enlighten your minds, and to instruct you how to worship the Great Spirit agreeably to his mind and will, and to preach to you the gospel of his son Jesus Christ. There is but one religion, and but one way to serve God, and if you do not embrace the right way, you cannot be happy hereafter. You have never worshipped the Great Spirit in a manner acceptable to him; but have, all your lives, been in great errors and darkness. To endeavor to remove these errors, and open your eyes, so that you might see clearly, is my business with you.

"*Brothers;* I wish to talk with you as one friend talks with another; and, if you have any objections to receive the religion which I preach, I wish you to state them; and I will endeavor to satisfy your minds, and remove the objections. . . .

"*Brothers;* Since I have been in this part of the country, I have visited some of your small villages, and talked with your people. They appear willing to receive instructions, but, as they look up to you as their older brothers in council, they want first to know your opinion on the subject.

"You have now heard what I have to propose at present. I hope you will take it into consideration, and give me an answer before we part.". . .

The Chief, commonly called by the white people, Red Jacket, (whose Indian name is Sagu-yu-what-hah, which interpreted is *Keeper awake*) rose and spoke as follows:

"*Friend and Brother;* It was the will of the Great Spirit that we should meet together this day. He orders all things, and has given us a fine day for our Council. He has taken his garment from before the sun, and caused it to shine with brightness upon us. Our eyes are opened, that we see clearly; our ears are unstopped, that we have been able to hear distinctly the words you have spoken. For all these favors we thank the Great Spirit; and Him *only*.

"*Brother;* This council fire was kindled by you. It was at your request that we came together at this time. We have listened with attention to what you have said. You requested us to speak our minds freely. This gives us great joy; for we now consider that we stand upright before you, and can speak what we think. All have heard your voice, and all speak to you now as one man. Our minds are agreed. . . .

"*Brother;* Listen to what we say.

"There was a time when our forefathers owned this great island. Their seats extended from the rising to the setting sun. The Great Spirit had made it for the use of Indians. He had created the buffalo, the deer, and other animals for food. He had made the bear and the beaver. Their skins served us for clothing. He had scattered them over the country, and taught us how to take them. He had caused the earth to produce corn for bread. All this He had done for his red children, because He loved them. If we had some disputes about our hunting ground, they were generally settled without the shedding of much blood. But an evil day came upon us. Your forefathers crossed the great water, and landed on this island. Their numbers were small. They found friends and not enemies. They told us they had fled from their own country for fear of wicked men, and had come here to enjoy their religion. They asked for a small seat. We took pity on them, granted their request; and they sat down amongst us. We gave them corn and meat, they gave us poison [alluding, it is supposed, to ardent spirits] in return.

"The white people had now found our country. Tidings were carried back, and more came amongst us. Yet we did not fear them.

We took them to be friends. They called us brothers. We believed them, and gave them a larger seat. At length their numbers had greatly increased. They wanted more land; they wanted our country. Our eyes were opened, and our minds became uneasy. Wars took place. Indians were hired to fight against Indians, and many of our people were destroyed. They also brought strong liquor amongst us. It was strong and powerful, and has slain thousands.

"*Brother*; Our seats were once large and yours were small. You have now become a great people, and we have scarcely a place left to spread our blankets. You have got our country, but are not satisfied; you want to force your religion upon us.

"*Brother*; Continue to listen.

"You say that you are sent to instruct us how to worship the Great Spirit agreeably to his mind, and, if we do not take hold of the religion which you white people teach, we shall be unhappy hereafter. You say that you are right and we are lost. How do we know this to be true? We understand that your religion is written in a book. If it was intended for us as well as you, why has not the Great Spirit given to us, and not only to us, but why did he not give to our forefathers, the knowledge of that book, with the means of understanding it rightly? We only know what you tell us about it. How shall we know when to believe, being so often deceived by the white people?

"*Brother*; You say there is but one way to worship and serve the Great Spirit. If there is but one religion; why do you white people differ so much about it? Why not all agreed, as you can all read the book?

"*Brother*; We do not understand these things.

"We are told that your religion was given to your forefathers, and has been handed down from father to son. We also have a religion, which was given to our forefathers, and has been handed down to us their children. We worship in that way. It teaches us to be thankful for all the favors we receive; to love each other, and to be united. We never quarrel about religion.

"*Brother*; The Great Spirit has made us all, but he has made a great difference between his white and red children. He has given us different complexions and different customs. To you He has given the arts. To these He has not opened our eyes. We know these things to be true. Since He has made so great a difference between us in other things, why may we not conclude that He has given us a different religion according to our understanding? The Great Spirit does right. He knows what is best for his children; we are satisfied.

"*Brother*; We do not wish to destroy your religion, or take it from you. We only want to enjoy our own. . . .

"*Brother*; You have now heard our answer to your talk, and this is all we have to say at present.

"As we are going to part, we will come and take you by the hand, and hope the Great Spirit will protect you on your journey, and return you safe to your friends."

As the Indians began to approach the missionary, he rose hastily from his seat and replied, that he could not take them by the hand; that there was no fellowship between the religion of God and the works of the devil.

This being interpreted to the Indians, they smiled, and retired in a peaceable manner.

Quoted in Wilcomb E. Washburn, ed., *The Indian and the White Man*. Garden City, NY: Doubleday, 1964, pp. 209–14.

Opposing Views of Land Ownership

Document 9: The Indians Were Here First

A common Native American view of land ownership is summed up in this excerpt from a speech given in 1810 by the legendary Shawnee warrior/orator Tecumseh to William H. Harrison, then governor of the Indiana Territory. The Indians have rights to the land, says Tecumseh, because they were its first occupants. And even if some of it was to be sold, all Indians, and not a single tribe, must agree to that sale.

It is true I am a Shawnee. My forefathers were warriors. Their son is a warrior. From them I only take my existence; from my tribe I take nothing. I am the maker of my own fortune; and oh! that I could make that of my red people, and of my country, as great as the conceptions of my mind, when I think of the Spirit that rules the universe. I would not then come to Governor Harrison, to ask him to tear the treaty, and to obliterate the landmark; but I would say to him, "Sir, you have liberty to return to your own country." The being within, communing with past ages, tells me, that once, nor until lately, there was no white man on this continent. That it then all belonged to red men, children of the same parents, placed on it by the Great Spirit that made them, to keep it, to traverse it, to enjoy its productions, and to fill it with the same race. Once a happy race. Since made miserable by the white people, who are never contented, but always encroaching. The way, and the only way to check and stop this evil, is, for all the red men to unite in claiming a common and equal right in the land, as it was at first, and should be yet; for it never was divided, but belongs to all, for the use of each. That no part has a right to sell, even to each other, much less to strangers, those who want all, and will not do with less. The white people have no right to take the land from the Indians, because they had it first; it is theirs. They may sell, but all must join. Any sale not made by all is not valid. The late sale is bad. It was made by a part only. Part do not know how to sell. It requires all to make a bargain for all. All red men have equal rights to the unoccupied land. The right of occupancy is as good in one place as in another. There cannot be two occupations in the same place. The first excludes all others. It is not so in hunting or traveling; for there the same ground will serve many, as they may follow each other all day; but the camp is stationary, and that is occupancy. It belongs to the first who sits down on his blanket or skins, which he has thrown upon the ground and till he leaves it no other has a right [to it].

Quoted in Annette Rosenstiel, *Red and White: Indian Views of the White Man, 1492–1982.* New York: Universe Books, 1983, p. 114.

Document 10: No Person Owns the Land

Another Native American view of land ownership—that no one owns and can dispose of the land except the Creator—is here presented by Chief Joseph, the great Nez Percé leader.

The earth was created by the assistance of the sun, and it should be left as it was. . . . The country was made without lines of demarcation, and it is no man's business to divide it. . . . I see the whites all over the country gaining wealth, and see their desire to give us lands which are worthless. . . . The earth and myself are of one mind. The measure of the land and the measure of our bodies are the same. Say to us if you can say it, that you were sent by the Creative Power to talk to us. Perhaps you think the Creator sent you here to dispose of us as you see fit. If I thought you were sent by the Creator I might be induced to think you had a right to dispose of me. Do not misunderstand me, but understand me fully with reference to my affection for the land. I never said the land was mine to do with it as I chose. The one who has the right to dispose of it is the one who has created it. I claim a right to live on my land, and accord you the privilege to live on yours.

Quoted in T.C. McLuhan, *Touch the Earth: A Self-Portrait of Indian Existence*. New York: Promontory Press, 1971, p. 54.

Document 11: Indians Had No Clear Title to the Land

The prevailing white view of Indian land ownership was that Indians only roamed over and hunted on the land; because they did not develop it, by creating permanent farms and cities on it as whites did, they did not own it. This presentation of the white argument is by Theodore Roosevelt, who became U.S. president shortly after the end of the Indians wars.

It is greatly to be wished that some competent person would write a full and true history of our national dealings with the Indians. Undoubtedly the latter have often suffered terrible injustice at our hands. A number of instances, such as the conduct of the Georgians to the Cherokees in the early part of the present century, or the whole treatment of Chief Joseph and his Nez Percés, might be mentioned, which are indelible blots on our fair fame; and yet, in describing our dealings with the red men as a whole, historians do us much less than justice.

It was wholly impossible to avoid conflicts with the weaker race, unless we were willing to see the American continent fall into the hands of some other strong power; and even had we adopted such a ludicrous policy, the Indians themselves would have made war upon us. It cannot be too often insisted that they did not own the land; or, at least, that their ownership was merely such as that claimed often by our own white hunters. If the Indians really owned Kentucky in 1775, then in 1776 it was the property of [frontiersman Daniel] Boon and his associates; and to dispossess one party was as great a wrong as to dispossess the other. To recognize the Indian ownership of the limitless prairies and forests of this continent—that is, to consider the dozen squalid savages who hunted at long intervals over a territory of a thousand square miles as owning it outright—necessarily implies a similar recognition of the claims of every white hunter, squatter, horse-thief, or wandering cattle-man. Take as an example the country round the Little Missouri. When the cattle-men, the first actual settlers, came into this land in 1882, it was already scantily peopled by a few white hunters and trappers. The latter were extremely jealous of intrusion; they had held their own in spite of the Indians, and, like the Indians, the inrush of settlers and the consequent destruction of the game meant their own undoing; also, again like the Indians, they felt that their having hunted over the soil gave them a vague prescriptive right to its sole occupation, and they did their best to keep actual settlers out. In some cases, to avoid difficulty, their nominal claims were bought up; generally, and rightly, they were disregarded. Yet they certainly had as good a right to the Little Missouri country as the Sioux have to most of the land on their present reservations. In fact, the mere statement of the case is sufficient to show the absurdity of asserting that the land really belonged to the Indians. The different tribes have always been utterly unable to define their own boundaries. Thus the Delawares and Wyandots, in 1785, though entirely separate nations, claimed and, in a certain sense, occupied almost exactly the same territory. . . .

Our government almost always tried to act fairly by the tribes; the governmental agents (some of whom have been dishonest, and others foolish, but who, as a class, have been greatly traduced), in their reports, are far more apt to be unjust to the whites than to the reds; and the Federal authorities, though unable to prevent much of the injustice, still did check and control the white borderers very much more effectually than the Indian sachems and war-chiefs controlled their young braves. The tribes were warlike and bloodthirsty, jealous of each other and of the whites; they claimed the land for their hunting grounds, but their claims all conflicted with one another; their knowledge of their own boundaries was so indefinite that they were always willing, for inadequate compensation, to sell land to which they had merely the vaguest title; and yet, when once they had received the goods, were generally reluctant to make over even what they could; they coveted the goods and scalps of the whites, and the young warriors were always on the alert to commit outrages when they could do it with impunity.

Theodore Roosevelt, *The Winning of the West* (first published 1889–1896), quoted in Wilcomb E. Washburn, ed., *The Indian and the White Man.* Garden City, NY: Doubleday, 1964, pp. 131–34.

Conflict Between Indians and Whites

Document 12: "We Should All Have to Die Fighting"
Black Elk, a renowned Sioux chief, here recalls the coming of the whites to his world, their exploitation of his people and resources, and the recognition that the Indians would have to fight for their own survival.

I can remember that winter of the hundred slain (1866) as a man may remember some bad dream he dreamed when he was little, but I can not tell just how much I heard when I was bigger and how much I understood when I was little. It is like some fearful thing in a fog, for it was a time when everything seemed troubled and afraid.

I had never seen a Wasichu [white man] then, and did not know what one looked like; but everyone was saying that the Wasichus were coming and that they were going to take our country and rub us all out and that we should all have to die fighting.

Once we were happy in our own country and we were seldom hungry, for then the two-leggeds and the four-leggeds lived together like relatives, and there was plenty for them and for us. But the Wasichus came, and they have made little islands for us and other little islands for the four-leggeds, and always these islands are becoming smaller, for around them surges the gnawing flood of the Wasichu; and it is dirty with lies and greed.

I was ten years old that winter, and that was the first time I ever saw a Wasichu. At first I thought they all looked sick, and I was afraid they might just begin to fight us any time, but I got used to them.

I can remember when the bison were so many that they could not be counted, but more and more Wasichus came to kill them until there were only heaps of bones scattered where they used to be. The Wasichus did not kill them to eat; they killed them for the metal that makes them crazy, and they took only the hides to sell. Sometimes they did not even take the hides, only the tongues; and I have heard that fire-boats came down the Missouri River loaded with dried bison tongues. You can see that the men who did this were crazy. Sometimes they did not even take the tongues; they just killed and killed because they liked to do that. When we hunted bison, we killed only what we needed.

Quoted in T.C. McLuhan, *Touch the Earth: A Self-Portrait of Indian Existence*. New York: Promontory Press, 1971, p. 71.

Document 13: Your Choice: Relocate or Face the Consequences

U.S. government demands for Indians to move, Indian defiance of these demands, and eventual forced removal formed a regularly repeated pattern in Indian-white conflict. This is part of the letter made public on April 7, 1835, in which President Andrew Jackson delivered what was in effect an ultimatum to the Cherokee then living in the Southeast to move west of the Mississippi. Jackson claimed that circumstances "beyond the reach of human laws" had made it impossible for the Cherokee to live any longer among "civilized" whites and threatened punishment if the tribe did not voluntarily leave. Some Cherokee did leave of their own accord. Those who refused were forcibly and cruelly relocated two years later.

To the Cherokee Tribe of Indians East of the Mississippi River:

My Friends: I have long viewed your condition with great interest. For many years I have been acquainted with your people, and under all variety of circumstances in peace and war. Your fathers were well known to me and the regard which I cherished for them has caused me to feel great solicitude for your situation. To these feelings, growing out of former recollections, have been added the sanction of official duty, and the relation in which, by the constitution and laws, I am placed towards you. Listen to me, therefore, as your fathers have listened, while I communicate to you my sentiments on the critical state of your affairs.

You are now placed in the midst of a white population . . . and you are now subject to the same laws which govern the other citizens of Georgia and Alabama. You are liable to prosecutions for offences, and to civil nations for a breach of any of your contracts. Most of your young people are uneducated, and are liable to be brought into collision at all times with their white neighbors. Your young men are acquiring habits of intoxication. With strong passions, and without those habits of restraint which our laws inculcate and render necessary, they are frequently driven to excesses which must eventually terminate in their ruin. The game has disappeared among you and you must depend upon agriculture and the mechanical arts for support. And, yet, a large portion of your people have acquired little or no property in the soil itself, or in any article of personal property which can be useful to them. How, under these circumstances, can you live in the country you now occupy? Your condition must become worse and worse, and you will ultimately disappear, as so many tribes have done before you.

Of all this I warned your people when I met them in council eighteen years ago. I then advised them to sell out their possessions east of the Mississippi and to remove to the country west of that river. This advice I have continued to give you at various times for that period down to the present day, and can you now look back and doubt the wisdom of this counsel? Had you then removed, you would have gone with all the means necessary to establish yourselves in a fertile country sufficiently extensive for your subsistence, and beyond the reach of the moral exile which are hastening your destruction. Instead of being a divided people as you now are arrayed into parties bitterly opposed to each other, you would have been a prosperous and a united community. Your farms would have been open and cultivated, comfortable houses would have been erected, the means of subsistence abundant, and you would have been governed by your own customs and laws, and removed from the effects of a white population. . . .

I have no motive, my friends, to deceive you. I am sincerely desirous to promote your welfare. Listen to me, therefore, while I tell you that you cannot remain where you now are. Circumstances that cannot be controlled, and which are beyond the reach of human laws, render it impossible that you can flourish in the midst of a civilized community. You have but one remedy within your reach. And that is, to remove to the West and join your countrymen, who are already established there. And the sooner you do this, the sooner you will commence your career of improvement and prosperity. . . .

The whole subject has been taken into consideration, and an arrangement has been made which ought to be, and I trust will be, entirely satisfactory to you. The Senate of the United States have given their opinion of the value of your possessions; and this value is ensured to you in the arrangement which has been prepared. . . . The stipulations contained in this instrument, are designed to afford due protection to private rights, to make adequate provision for the poorer class of your people, to provide for the removal of all, and lay the foundation of such social and political establishments in your new country as will render you a happy and prosperous people. Why, then, should any honest man among you object to removal? The United States have assigned to you a fertile and extensive country, with a very fine climate adapted to your habits, and with all the other natural advantages which you ought to desire or expect.

I shall, in the course of a short time, appoint commissioners for the purpose of meeting the whole body of your people in council. They will explain to you, more fully, my views, and the nature of the stipulations which are offered to you.

These stipulations provide:

1st. For an addition to the country already assigned to the west of Mississippi, and for the conveyance of the whole of it, by patent, in fee simple. And also for the security of the necessary political rights and for preventing white persons from trespassing upon you.

2nd. For the payment of the full value of each individual, of his possessions in Georgia, Alabama, North Carolina, and Tennessee.

3rd. For the removal, at the expense of the United States, of your whole people; for their subsistence for one year after their arrival in their new country, and for a gratuity of one hundred and fifty dollars to each person.

4th. For the usual supply of rifles, blankets, and kettles.

5th. For the investment of the sum of four hundred thousand dollars, in order to secure a permanent annuity.

6th. For adequate provision for schools, agricultural instruments, domestic animals, missionary establishments, the support of orphans, &c.

7th. For the payment of claims.

8th. For granting pensions to such of your people as have been disabled in the service of the United States. . . .

The choice now is before you. May the Great Spirit teach you how to choose. The fate of your women and children, the fate of your people to the remotest generation, depend upon the issue. Deceive yourselves no longer. Do not cherish the belief that you can ever resume your former political situation, while you continue in your present residence. As certain as the sun shines to guide you in your path, so certain is it that you cannot drive back the laws of Georgia from among you. Every year will increase your difficulties. Look how their young men are committing depredations upon the property of our citizens, and are shedding their blood. This cannot and will not be allowed. Punishment will follow, and all who are engaged in these offences must suffer. Your young men will commit the same acts, and the same consequences must ensue.

Think then of all these things. Shut your ears to bad counsels. Look at your condition as it now is, and then consider what it will be if you follow the advice I give you.

Your friend, Andrew Jackson—Washington, March 16, 1835.

Quoted in John Ehle, *Trail of Tears: The Rise and Fall of the Cherokee Nation.* New York: Doubleday, 1988, pp. 275–78.

Document 14: Indian Modes of Warfare Highly Efficient

When engaged in battle for the first time with Indians, many whites were surprised at the effectiveness of Indian fighting methods. This excerpt from a 1799 account by Colonel James Smith of Kentucky, who both fought and studied Indians, praises Indian discipline, courage, and fighting abilities, and recommends that white soldiers learn to imitate their red enemies.

I have often heard the British officers call the Indians the undisciplined savages, which is a capital mistake—as they have all the essentials of discipline. They are under good command, and punctual in obeying orders: they can act in concert, and when their officers lay a plan and give orders, they will cheerfully unite in putting all their directions into immediate execution; and by each man observing the motion or movement of his right hand companion, they can communicate the motion from right to left, and march abreast in concert, and in scattered order, though the line may be more than a mile long, and continue, if occasion requires, for a considerable distance, without disorder or confusion. They can perform various necessary manoeuvres, either slowly, or as fast as they can run: they can form a circle, or semi-circle: the circle they make use of, in order to surround their enemy, and the semi-circle, if the enemy has a river on one side of them. They can also form a large hollow square, face out and take trees: this they do, if their enemies are about surrounding them, to prevent being shot from either side of the tree. When they go into battle, they are not loaded or encumbered with many clothes, as they commonly fight naked, save only breech-clout, leggins and moccasins. There is no such thing as corporeal punishment used, in order to bring them under such good discipline: degrading is the only chastisement, and they are so unanimous in this, that it effectually answers the purpose. Their officers plan, order and conduct matters until they are brought into action, and then each man is to fight as though he was to gain the battle himself. General orders are commonly given in time of battle, either to advance or retreat, and is done by a shout or yell, which is well understood, and then they retreat or advance in concert. They are generally well equipped, and exceedingly expert and active in the use of arms. . . .

Nothing can be more unjustly represented, than the different accounts we have had of their number from time to time, both by their own computations, and that of the British. While I was among them, I saw the account of the number, that they in those parts gave to the French, and kept it by me. When they in their own council-house, were taking an account of their number, with a piece of bark newly stripped, and a small stick, which answered the end of a slate and pencil, I took an account of the different nations and tribes, which I added together, and found there were not half the number, which they had given the French; and though they were then their allies, and lived among them, it was not easy finding out the deception, as they were a wandering set, and some of them almost always in the woods hunting. I asked one of the chiefs what was their reason for making such different returns? He said it was for political reasons, in order to obtain greater presents from the French, by telling them they could not divide such and such quantities of goods among so many. . . .

Though large volumes have been written on morality yet it may be all summed up in saying, do as you would wish to be done by: so the Indians sum up the art of war in the following manner:

The business of the private warriors is to be under command, or punctually to obey orders; to learn to march abreast in scattered order, so as to be in readiness to surround the enemy, or to prevent being surrounded; to be good marksmen, and active in the use of arms; to practice running; to learn to endure hunger or hardships with patience and fortitude; to tell the truth at all times to their officers, but more especially when sent out to spy the enemy.

Concerning Officers.—They say that it would be absurd to appoint a man an officer whose skill and courage had never been tried—that all officers should be advanced only according to merit; that no one man should have the absolute command of an army; that a council of officers are to determine when, and how an attack is to be made; that it is the business of the officers to lay plans to take every advantage of the enemy, to ambush and surprise them, and to prevent being ambushed and surprised themselves. It is the duty of officers to prepare and deliver speeches to the men, in order to animate and encourage them; and on the march, to prevent the men, at any time, from getting into a huddle, because if the enemy should surround them in this position, they would be exposed to the enemy's fire. It is likewise their business at all times to endeavour to annoy their enemy, and save their own men, and therefore ought never to bring on an attack without considerable advantage, or without what appeared to them the sure prospect of victory, and that with the loss of few men; and if at any time they should be mistaken in this, and are like to lose many men by gaining the victory, it is their duty to retreat, and wait for a better opportunity of defeating their enemy, without the danger of losing so many men. Their conduct proves that they act upon these principles, therefore . . . they have seldom ever made an unsuccessful attack. . . . They will commonly retreat if their men are falling fast; they will not stand cutting like the Highlanders or other British troops; but this proceeds from a compliance with their rules of war rather than cowardice. If they are surrounded they will fight while there is a man of them alive, rather than surrender. When Colonel

John Armstrong surrounded the Cattanyan town, on the Al-
legheny river, Captain Jacobs, a Delaware chief, with some warriors, took possession of a house, defended themselves for some
time, and killed a number of our men. As Jacobs could speak English, our people called on him to surrender. He said, that he and
his men were warriors, and they would all fight while life remained. He was again told that they should be well used if they
would only surrender; and if not, the house should be burned
down over their heads. Jacobs replied, he could eat fire; and when
the house was in a flame, he, and they that were with him, came
out in a fighting position, and were all killed. As they are a sharp,
active kind of people, and war is their principal study, in this they
have arrived at considerable perfection. We may learn of the Indians what is useful and laudable, and at the same time lay aside their
barbarous proceedings. . . .

Why have we not made greater proficiency in the Indian art of
war? Is it because we are too proud to imitate them, even though it
should be a means of preserving the lives of many of our citizens?
No! We are not above borrowing language from them, such as
homony, pone, tomahawk, &c. which is of little or no use to us. I ap-
prehend, that the reasons why we have not improved more in this
respect are as follow: no important acquisition is to be obtained but
by attention and diligence; and as it is easier to learn to move and act
in concert, in close order, in the open plain, than to act in concert in
scattered order in the woods, so it is easier to learn our discipline
than the Indian manoeuvres. They train up their boys in the art of
war from the time they are twelve or fourteen years of age; whereas,
the principal chance our people had of learning was, by observing
their manoeuvres when in action against us. I have been long astonished that no one has written upon this important subject, as their
art of war would not only be of use to us in case of another rupture
with them; but were only part of our men taught this art, accompanied with our continental discipline, I think no European power,
after trial, would venture to show its head in the American woods.

An Account of the Remarkable Occurrences in the Life and Travels of Colonel James Smith (from an
1831 edition), quoted in Wilcomb E. Washburn, ed., *The Indian and the White Man.* Garden
City, NY: Doubleday, 1964, pp. 261–69.

Document 15: The Sioux Victory at the Rosebud

*The defeat of George Custer by the Sioux and their allies at the Little
Bighorn on June 25, 1876, usually comes to mind when people think*

about Indian battles, especially Indian victories. Few people today are aware that the Sioux delivered U.S. troops another major defeat about a week before (June 17) at Rosebud Creek, a few miles east of the Little Bighorn. Following are excerpts from the detailed eyewitness account written on July 6 by Reuben B. Davinport, a correspondent for the New York Herald, *who fought in the Rosebud battle under the command of General George Crook.*

Three days ago the first fight of the campaign against the Sioux in this military department took place. The fighting column marched from the camp, situated at the fork of Goose Creek, on June 16, accompanied by the 250 Indian auxiliaries who had arrived on the preceding day, and numbered about 1,300 men. The infantry were mounted upon mules borrowed from the pack trains. Twenty mounted packers were also allowed to go, and carried carbines. The cavalry battalions contained 832 able soldiers. The friendly Indians were loaned firearms belonging to the government and their belts filled with cartridges. Old Crow was the principal leader of the Crows, and Medicine Crow and Good Heart his lieutenants. . . . After crossing the sterile hills and leaving behind them stunted thorns and cedars the column stretched like a great serpent over a green divide, whose surface is undulating as billows of mid-ocean, and which separates the watersheds of the Tongue River and the Rosebud Creek. The country is beautiful. The march was silent as possible, and the column was dispersed so as to avoid causing dust, which might give warning to the enemy. It was hoped to approach within thirty miles of the Sioux village and then to advance on it during the night.

After a weary march of thirty-five miles the column bivouacked at the head of the valley of the Rosebud on June 16. The soldiers placed their blankets so that in sleeping their lines formed a hollow square, inside of which the animals were picketed.

On the morning of June 17 the command moved at five o'clock. The Crow scouts went in front and on the flanks, but they had omitted to send forward their spies during the night, although on the previous day they had found indubitable signs that the Sioux were then engaged in hunting the buffalo southward. About half-past seven an advance of ten miles had been made, when, suddenly, the Old Crow appeared on a hill near the stream, and gave a signal. Soon other scouts dashed into the valley. Meanwhile the Crows were catching their war ponies, stripping off their superfluous garments, and some of them had formed in line and were singing their war song. A halt had been made at the first signal of the scouts, and the order was given to unsaddle the animals, it being supposed that they had merely seen some of the Sioux, near their village upon the hills, engaged in herding their ponies. The two battalions of the Third cavalry were resting on the south side of the creek and the one of the Second on the north side. Suddenly yells were heard beyond the low hill on the north, and shots were fired, which every moment were becoming more frequent. The Crows were wild with excitement, and shouted to the interpreters that their scouts were being killed and that they must go to join them. After circling on their ponies in the valley for ten minutes they dashed over the hill and disappeared. The firing became more and more rapid. The cavalry were making ready to mount, when scouts came galloping back again, hallooing that the Sioux were charging.

General Crook rode to the first crest and saw that they were coming forward to attack the whole command in the valley. Orders were given Colonel [Lieutenant Colonel William B.] Royall to lead the battalions of the Third cavalry across the stream, deploy his troops as skirmishers and occupy the hills in the possession of the enemy. Captain [Guy V.] Henry's battalion of the Third cavalry, consisting of Companies D, B, L and F, advanced northward up a series of ridges occupied by the Indians, who retired before the steady charge from point to point. At last was reached the top of a ridge lying adjacent to the highest crest, but separated from it by a deep ravine. The Sioux were in front and were promptly attacked. . . .

Seeing the long gallant skirmish line [of soldiers] pause, however, they dashed forward on the right and left, and in an instant nearly every point of vantage within, in front and in the rear, and on the flank of the line, was covered with savages wildly circling their ponies and charging hither and thither, while they fired from their seats with wonderful rapidity and accuracy.

At this moment the loss to the troops commenced. They opened a severe fire upon the Indians, which was seen to have instant effect, but a cry arose that they were the Crows, and immediately it was checked. Thus was lost an excellent opportunity for punishing them severely. They screened themselves behind elevations and continued a harassing fire. Still the troops on the right did not advance, and the suspense grew terrible as the position was every moment more perilous as the Sioux appeared at intervals on the left flank, charging on their ponies and each time further toward the rear. . . .

At this juncture the soldiers felt great discouragement, but preserved their coolness although death had just begun his work among them, a murderous enfilading fire causing them to drop every moment. Captain [Peter D.] Vroom, Lieutenant [Charles] Morton and Lieutenant [Henry R.] Lemley [Lemly] of the Third cavalry took places in the skirmish line when the enemy were within range and used their carbines with effect. Unwilling to let slip an opportunity for helping the extrication of the left line with which my own fate was identified by the chance of battle, I dismounted at several points during our retreat and fired with the skirmishers. At last when the receding line reached the last ridge next the fatal hollow it became evident that the sacrifice of a few lives was inevitable for the salvation of many more. Colonel Royall sent his adjutant Lieutenant Lemley through the storm of bullets to ask a support of infantry to protect his retreat. About the same moment Captain Guy V. Henry who had remained at the head of his battalion under the hottest fire was horribly wounded in the face. He was lifted from his horse and led to the rear by two of his soldiers. The tide of retreat now grew more excited and turbulent and I was pressed back with the soldier attending me over the rearward crest upon the slope which was raked by an oblique fire from the north.

The infantry which was expected to relieve this line was not in position soon enough to check the wild advance of the Sioux, who, observing the retiring body becoming crowded together on the edge of the gap which it must cross under fire, rushed both down and up the valley on the right while they poured their fire from the high bluff across the low elevation, rendering it utterly untenable, while they were charging at the same time to prevent its abandonment. A swarm of Sioux were within 1,000 yards of me in front and I heard their shots in the rear as they murdered the poor soldiers of the rear guard of the retreat. I was obliged either to take the chance of death then or wait to cross with the battalion, which would attract a still more fatal fire, because it would form a large mark for the aim of the enemy. The hill where the General's headquarters were and a large body of troops which had not yet been engaged was more than half a mile distant. I chose the converging ravines and rode through them a greater part of the way, but as I galloped up the slope opposite the one I had left I heard the yells of the savages close behind, and the reports of their rifles, as I emerged from the safer ground, sounded remarkably near and loud.

Looking behind I saw a dozen Sioux surrounding a group of soldiers who had straggled behind the retreat. Six were killed at one spot. A recruit surrendered his carbine to a painted warrior, who flung it to the ground and cleft his head with a stroke of the tomahawk. William W. Allen, a brave old soldier who had been twenty years in the army, fought with magnificent courage and was killed. The Sioux rode so close to their victims that they shot them in the face with revolvers and the powder blackened the flesh. . . . About the same time a corporal of F company, of the Third cavalry, made a last charge with three men, and captured from the enemy the bodies of their comrades, thus saving them from the scalping knife.

Quoted in Jerome A. Greene, ed., *Battles and Skirmishes of the Great Sioux War, 1876–1877: A Military View*. Norman: University of Oklahoma Press, 1993, pp. 26–34.

Document 16: Treat All Men Alike

This powerful and moving statement was delivered by Chief Joseph, the Nez Percé leader, to a large group of government officials in Washington, D.C., in 1879. The chief bitterly criticizes government lies, broken promises, and maintenance of a double standard for whites and Indians. As scholar Annette Rosenstiel points out, Joseph's words and manner foreshadow the outspoken complaints voiced by militant Indian activists in the twentieth century.

I have shaken hands with a great many friends, but there are some things I want to know which no one seems able to explain. I cannot understand how the Government sends out a man to fight us, as it did General [Nelson A.] Miles, and then breaks his word. [General Miles had promised that if Joseph surrendered, his people would be returned to their own part of the country; instead they had been sent to Fort Leavenworth, Kansas.] Such a government has something wrong about it. I cannot understand why so many chiefs are allowed to talk so many different ways, and promise so many different things. I have seen the Great Father Chief [President Rutherford B. Hayes] . . . and many other law chiefs [congressmen], and they all say they are my friends, and that I shall have justice, but while their mouths all talk right I do not understand why nothing is done for my people. I have heard talk and talk, but nothing is done. Good words do not last long unless they amount to something. Words do not pay for my dead people. They do not pay for my country, now overrun by white men. They do not protect my father's grave. They do not pay for all my horses and cattle. Good words will not give me back my children. Good words will not make good the promise of your War chief General Miles. Good words will not give my people good health and stop them from dying. Good words will not get my people a home where they can live in peace and take care of themselves. I am tired of talk that comes to nothing. It makes my heart sick when I remember all the good words and all the broken promises. There has been too much talking by men who had no right to talk. Too many misrepresentations have been made, too many misunderstandings have come up between the white men about the Indians. If the white man wants to live in peace with the Indian he can live in peace. There need be no trouble. Treat all men alike. Give them the same law. Give them an even chance to live and grow. All men were made by the same Great Spirit Chief. They are all brothers. The earth is the mother of all people, and all people should have equal rights upon it. You might as well expect the rivers to run backward as that any man who was born a free man should be contented when penned up and denied liberty to go where he pleases. If you tie a horse to a stake, do you expect he will grow fat? If you pen an Indian up on a small spot of earth, and compel him to stay there, he will not be contented, nor will he grow and prosper. I have asked some of the great white chiefs where they get their authority to say to the Indian that he shall stay in one place, while he sees white men going where they please. They cannot tell me.

I only ask of the government to be treated as all other men are treated. If I cannot go to my own home, let me have a home in some country where my people will not die so fast. . . .

When I think of our condition my heart is heavy. I see men of my race treated as outlaws and driven from country to country or shot down like animals.

I know that my race must change. We cannot hold our own with white men as we are. We ask only an even chance to live as other men live. We ask to be recognized as men. We ask that the same law shall work alike on all men. If the Indian breaks the law, punish him by the law. If the white man breaks the law, punish him also.

Let me be a free man—free to travel, free to stop, free to work, free to trade where I choose, free to choose my own teachers, free to follow the religion of my fathers, free to think and talk and act for myself—and I will obey every law, or submit to the penalty.

Whenever the white man treats an Indian as they treat each other, then we will have no more wars. We shall all be alike—brothers of one father and one mother, with one mother, with one sky above us and one country around us, and one government for all. Then the Great Spirit Chief who rules above will smile upon this land, and send rain to wash out the bloody spots made by brothers' hands from the face of the earth. For this time the Indian race are waiting and praying. I hope that no more groans of wounded men and women will ever go to the ear of the Great Spirit Chief above, and that all people may be one people.

In-mut-too-yah-lat-lat [Chief Joseph] has spoken for his people.

Quoted in Annette Rosenstiel, *Red and White: Indian Views of the White Man, 1492–1982.* New York: Universe Books, 1983, pp. 142–45.

Document 17: The Whites Will Sink into the Earth

The sad finale of the American Indian wars took place at Wounded Knee in 1890, amid the spread of the Ghost Dance religion across the western plains. In this lecture, given in October 1890, Short Bull, a Sioux, assures his followers that, if they carefully observe the rituals, they will succeed in destroying the whites.

Now, there will be a tree sprout up, and there all the members of our religion and the tribe must gather together. That will be the place where we will see our dead relations. But before this time we must dance the balance of this moon, at the end of which time the earth will shiver very hard. Whenever this thing occurs, I will start the wind to blow. We are the ones who will then see our fathers, mothers, and everybody. We, the tribe of Indians, are the ones who are living a sacred life. God, our father himself, has told and commanded and shown me to do these things.

Our father in heaven has placed a mark at each point of the four winds. First, a clay pipe, which lies at the setting of the sun and represents the Sioux tribe. Second, there is a holy arrow lying at the north, which represents the Cheyenne tribe. Third, at the rising of the sun there lies hail, representing the Arapaho tribe. Fourth, there lies a pipe and nice feather at the south, which represents the Crow tribe. My father has shown me these things, therefore we must continue this dance. If the soldiers surround you four deep, three of you, on whom I have put holy shirts, will sing a song, which I have taught you, around them, when some of them will drop dead. Then the rest will start to run, but their horses will sink into the earth. The riders will jump from their horses, but they will sink into the earth also. Then you can do as you desire with them. Now, you must know this, that all the soldiers and that race will be dead. There will be only five thousand of them left living on the earth. My friends and relations, this is straight and true.

Now, we must gather at Pass Creek where the tree is sprouting. There we will go among our dead relations. You must not take any earthly things with you. Then the men must take off all their clothing and the women must do the same. No one shall be ashamed of exposing their persons. My father above has told us to do this, and we must do as he says. You must not be afraid of anything. The guns are the only things we are afraid of, but they belong to our father in heaven. He will see that they do not harm. Whatever white men may tell you, do not listen to them, my relations. This is all. I will now raise my hand up to my father and close what he has said to you through me.

Quoted in Edward H. Spicer, *A Short History of the Indians of the United States.* New York: D. Van Nostrand, 1969, pp. 282–83.

U.S. Indian Policy and Legislation

Document 18: The General Allotment Act

This act, also referred to as the Dawes Act, passed in 1887, provided for dividing up Indian reservations into tiny land parcels, to be "allotted" to Indian families. In keeping with the then prevailing white policy of assimilation, the U.S. government hoped that giving Indians a taste of "real" land ownership would "civilize" them. The bill also allowed the government to sell off pieces of the reservations to white settlers, a process that significantly reduced the size of Indian lands in subsequent decades.

An act to provide for the allotment of lands in severally to Indians on the various reservations, and to extend the protection of the laws of the United States and the Territories over the Indians, and for other purposes.

Be it enacted by the Senate and House of Representatives of the United States of America in Congress assembled, That in all cases where any tribe or band of Indians has been, or shall hereafter be, located upon any reservation created for their use, either by treaty stipulation or by virtue of an act of Congress or Executive order setting apart the same for their use, the President of the United States be, and he hereby is, authorized, whenever in his opinion any reservation or any part thereof of such Indians is advantageous for agricultural and grazing purposes, to cause said reservation, or any part thereof, to be surveyed, or resurveyed if necessary, and to allot the lands in said reservation in severally to any Indian located thereon in quantities as follows:

To each head of a family, one-quarter of a section;

To each single person over eighteen years of age, one-eighth of a section;

To each orphan child under eighteen years of age, one-eighth of a section. . . .

SEC. 2. That all allotments set apart under the provisions of this act shall be selected by the Indians, heads of families selecting for their minor children, and the agents shall select for each orphan child, and in such manner as to embrace the improvements of the Indians making the selection. Where the improvements of two or more Indians have been made on the same legal subdivision of land, unless they shall otherwise agree, a provisional line may be run dividing said lands between them, and the amount to which each is entitled shall be equalized in the assignment of the remainder of the land to which they are entitled under this act: *Provided*, That if any one entitled to an allotment shall fail to make a selection within four years after the President shall direct that allotments may be made on a particular reservation, the Secretary of the Interior may direct the agent of such tribe or band, if such there be, and if there be no agent, then a special agent appointed for that purpose, to make a selection for such Indian, which selection shall be allotted as in cases where selections are made by the Indians, and patents shall issue in like manner. . . .

SEC. 4. That where any Indian not residing upon a reservation, or for whose tribe no reservation has been provided by treaty, act of Congress, or Executive order, shall make settlement upon any surveyed or unsurveyed lands of the United States not otherwise appropriated, he or she shall be entitled, upon application to the local land office for the district in which the lands are located, to have the same allotted to him or her, and to his or her children, in quantities and manner as provided in this act for Indians residing upon reservations. . . .

SEC. 5. That upon the approval of the allotments provided for in this act by the Secretary of the Interior, he shall cause patents to issue therefore in the name of the allottees, which patents shall be of the legal effect, and declare that the United States does and will hold the land thus allotted, for the period of twenty-five years, in trust for the sole use and benefit of the Indian to whom such allotment shall have been made, or, in case of his decease, of his heirs according to the laws of the State or Territory where such land is located. . . . *And provided further,* That at any time after lands have been allotted to all the Indians of any tribe as herein provided, or sooner if in the opinion of the President it shall be for the best interests of said tribe, it shall be lawful for the Secretary of the Interior to negotiate with such Indian tribe for the purchase and release by said tribe, in conformity with the treaty or statute under which such reservation is held, of such portions of its reservation not allotted as such tribe shall, from time to time, consent to sell, on such terms and conditions as shall be considered just and equitable between the United States and said tribe of Indians, which purchase shall not be complete until ratified by Congress, and the form and manner of executing such release shall also be prescribed by Congress: *Provided, however,* That all lands adapted to agriculture, with or without irrigation, so sold or released to the United States by any Indian tribe shall be held by the United States for the sole purpose of securing homes to actual settlers and shall be disposed of by the United States to actual and bona fide settlers only in tracts not exceeding one hundred and sixty acres to any one person, on such terms as Congress shall prescribe. . . .

SEC. 6. That upon the completion of said allotments and the patenting of the lands to said allottees, each and every member of the respective bands or tribes of Indians to whom allotments have been made shall have the benefit of and be subject to the laws, both civil and criminal, of the State or Territory in which they may reside; and no Territory shall pass or enforce any law denying any such Indian within its jurisdiction the equal protection of the law. And every Indian born within the territorial limits of the United States to whom allotments shall have been made under the provisions of this act, or under any law or treaty, and every Indian born within the territorial limits of the United States who has voluntarily taken up, within said limits, his residence separate and apart from any tribe of Indians therein, and has adopted the habits of civilized life, is hereby declared to be a citizen of the United States, and is entitled to all the rights, privileges, and immunities of such citizens, whether said Indian has been or not, by birth or otherwise a member of any tribe of Indians within the territorial limits of the United States, without in any manner impairing or otherwise affecting the right of any such Indian to tribal or other property. . . .

SEC. 8. That the provisions of this act shall not extend to the territory occupied by the Cherokees, Creeks, Choctaws, Chickasaws, Seminoles, and Osage, Miamies and Peorias, and Sacs and

Foxes, in the Indian Territory, nor to any of the reservations of the Seneca Nation of New York Indians in the State of New York, nor to that strip of territory in the State of Nebraska adjoining the Sioux Nation on the south added by Executive order. . . .

SEC. 10. That nothing in this act contained shall be so construed as to affect the right and power of Congress to grant the right of way through any lands granted to an Indian, or a tribe of Indians, for railroads or other highways, or telegraph lines, for the public use, or to condemn such lands to public uses, upon making just compensation.

Quoted in Edward H. Spicer, *A Short History of the Indians of the United States*. New York: D. Van Nostrand, 1969, pp. 200–204.

Document 19: Indians Protest the General Allotment Act

This protest against the General Allotment Act, addressed to the president of the United States, was filed in 1895 by representatives of the Choctaw and Chickasaw tribes. Their bitter words demonstrate that most Indians did not want to become U.S. citizens or whitelike homesteaders or otherwise be assimilated into white society and thereby lose their Native American identity.

We desire to recall a little history of our people. The Choctaw and Chickasaw people have never cost the United States a cent for support. They have always and are now self-sustaining. It will be admitted that but little over a half a century ago the Choctaws and Chickasaws were happily located east of the Mississippi River. Their possessions were large and rich and valuable. The whites began to crowd around and among us in the east, as they now are in the west. The Government of the United States urged us to relinquish our valuable possessions there to make homes for their own people and to accept new reservations west of the great river Mississippi, assuring us that there we would be secure from the invasion of the white man. Upon condition that the Government would protect us from such renewed invasion and would . . . by solemn treaty guarantee that no Territorial or State Government should ever be extended over us without consent . . . we consented, and with heavy hearts we turned our backs upon the graves of our fathers and took up the dismal march for our new western home, in a wilderness west of the Mississippi River. . . .

In 1855, at the request of the United States we leased and sold the entire west part of our reservation amounting to over 12 mil-

lion acres, for the purpose of homes for the white man and of lo-
cating thereon other friendly Indians. Again in 1866, at the urgent
request of the Government we gave up all that part leased for the
occupancy of friendly Indians, and ceded it absolutely for the same
purpose. And again, in 1890 and 1891, we relinquished . . . 3 million acres . . . to be occupied by the whites. Now in less than five
years we are asked to surrender completely our tribal governments
and to accept a Territorial Government in lieu thereof; to allot our
lands in severally, and to become citizens of the United States and
what is worse, an effort is being made to force us to do so against
our consent. Such a radical change would, in our judgement, in a
few years annihilate the Indian. . . .

We ask every lover of justice, is it right that a great and powerful government should, year by year, continue to demand cessions
of land from weaker and dependent people, under the plea of securing homes for the homeless? While the great government of
the United States, our guardian, is year by year admitting foreign
paupers into the Union, at the rate of 250,000 per annum, must we
sacrifice our homes and children for this pauper element?

We have lived with our people all our lives and believe that we
know more about them than any Commission, however good and
intelligent, could know from a few visits . . . on the railroads and
towns, where but a few Indians are to be seen and where but few
live. . . . They [the white man] care nothing for the fate of the Indian, so that their own greed can be gratified.

Quoted in T.C. McLuhan, *Touch the Earth: A Self-Portrait of Indian Existence*. New York:
Promontory Press, 1971, pp. 96–97.

Document 20: The Indian Reorganization Act

*This act, passed in 1934 and excerpted here, reversed the allotment pol-
icy established in the closing years of the nineteenth century. The new bill
not only reestablished the physical integrity of the reservations as large,
undivided tracts, but also allowed the tribes to set up their own local governments. In addition, the act introduced federal programs supporting
economic development and vocational education on the reservations.*

> To conserve and develop Indian lands and resources; to extend to Indians
> the right to form business and other organizations; to establish a credit sys-
> tem for Indians; to grant certain rights of home rule to Indians; to provide
> for vocational education for Indians; and for other purposes.

Be it enacted by the Senate and House of Representatives of the

United States of America in Congress assembled, That hereafter no land of any Indian reservation, created or set apart by treaty or agreement with the Indians, Act of Congress, Executive order, purchase, or otherwise, shall be allotted in severally to any Indian.

Section 2. The existing periods of trust placed upon any Indian lands and any restriction on alienation thereof are hereby extended and continued until otherwise directed by Congress.

Section 3. The Secretary of the Interior, if he shall find it to be in the public interest, is hereby authorized to restore to tribal ownership the remaining surplus lands of any Indian reservation heretofore opened, or authorized to be opened, to sale, or any other form of disposal by Presidential proclamation, or by any of the public-land laws of the United States. . . .

Section 4. Except as herein provided, no sale, devise, gift, exchange or other transfer of restricted Indian lands or of shares in the assets of any Indian tribe or corporation organized hereunder, shall be made or approved: Provided, however, That such lands or interests may, with the approval of the Secretary of the Interior, be sold, devised, or otherwise transferred to the Indian tribe in which the lands or shares are located or from which the shares were derived or to a successor corporation; and in all instances such lands or interests shall descend or be devised, in accordance with the then existing laws of the State, or Federal laws where applicable; in which said lands are located or in which the subject matter of the corporation is located, to any member of such tribe or of such corporation or any heirs of such member. . . .

Section 9. There is hereby authorized to be appropriated, out of any funds in the Treasury not otherwise appropriated, such sums as may be necessary, but not to exceed $250,000 in any fiscal year, to be expended at the order of the Secretary of the Interior, in defraying the expenses of organizing Indian chartered corporations or other organizations created under this Act.

Section 10. There is hereby authorized to be appropriated, out of any funds in the Treasury not otherwise appropriated, the sum of $10,000,000 to be established as a revolving fund from which the Secretary of the Interior, under such rules and regulations as he may prescribe, may make loans to Indian chartered corporations for the purpose of promoting the economic development of such tribes and of their members, and may defray the expenses of administering such loans. Repayment of amounts loaned under this authorization shall be credited to the revolving fund and shall be available for the purposes for which the fund is established. . . .

Section 11. There is hereby authorized to be appropriated, out of any funds in the United States Treasury not otherwise appropriated, a sum not to exceed $25,000 annually, together with any unexpended balances of previous appropriations made pursuant to this section, for loans to Indians for the payment of tuition and other expenses in recognized vocational and trade schools. . . .

Section 15. Nothing in this Act shall be construed to impair or prejudice any claim or suit of any Indian tribe against the United States. It is hereby declared to be the intent of Congress that no expenditures for the benefit of Indians made out of appropriations authorized by this Act shall be considered as offsets in any suit brought to recover upon any claim of such Indians against the United States.

Section 16. Any Indian tribe or tribes, residing on the same reservation, shall have the right to organize for its common welfare, and may adopt an appropriate constitution and bylaws, which shall become effective when ratified by a majority vote of the adult members of the tribe, or of the adult Indians residing on such reservation, as the case may be, at a special election authorized and called by the Secretary of the Interior under such rules and regulations as he may prescribe. Such constitution and bylaws when ratified as aforesaid and approved by the Secretary of the Interior shall be revocable by an election open to the same voters and conducted in the same manner as hereinabove provided. . . .

In addition to all powers vested in any Indian tribe or tribal council by existing law, the constitution adopted by said tribe shall also vest in such tribe or its tribal council the following rights and powers: To employ legal counsel, the choice of counsel and fixing of fees to be subject to the approval of the Secretary of the Interior; to prevent the sale, disposition, lease, or encumbrance of tribal lands, interests in lands, or other tribal assets without the consent of the tribe; and to negotiate with the Federal, State, and local Governments. The Secretary of the Interior shall advise such tribe or its tribal council of all appropriation estimates or Federal projects for the benefit of the tribe prior to the submission of such estimates to the Bureau of the Budget and the Congress. . . .

Section 19. The term "Indian" as used in this Act shall include all persons of Indian descent who are members of any recognized Indian tribe now under Federal jurisdiction, and all persons who are descendants of such members who were, on June 1, 1934, residing within the present boundaries of any Indian reservation, and shall further include all other persons of one-half or more Indian blood. . . . The term "tribe" wherever used in this Act shall be construed to refer to any Indian tribe, organized band, pueblo, or the Indians residing on one reservation. The words "adult Indians" wherever used in this Act shall be construed to refer to Indians who have attained the age of twenty one years.

Approved, June 18, 1934.

Quoted in Edward H. Spicer, *A Short History of the Indians of the United States.* New York: D. Van Nostrand, 1969, pp. 212–17.

Chronology

1607
About nine hundred English settlers establish the colony of Jamestown, on the shore of Chesapeake Bay in what is now Virginia. They are greeted and aided by the local Indians.

1620
Members of the Massasoit tribe assist new settlers landing in Massachusetts.

1743
Thomas Jefferson, who will later advocate moving eastern Indian tribes across the Mississippi, is born in Virginia.

1754–1763
The French and Indian War, fought between Britain and France and their respective colonists and Indian allies.

1756–1757
The Delaware tribe battles encroaching whites on the Pennsylvania frontier.

1759–1760
The Cherokee fight with white settlers on the Carolina frontier.

1768
Tecumseh, the noted Shawnee advocate of Indian unity, is born near the present site of Springfield, Ohio.

1775–1783
The American Revolution. In 1776, the British colonists declare their independence from the mother country, giving birth to the United States.

1790
The Shawnee, Miami, and other tribes join forces under Tecumseh and Little Turtle to defeat an army of fourteen hundred U.S. troops in the Ohio Valley. The same Indians defeat another U.S. force the following year.

1794

General Anthony Wayne defeats Tecumseh in the Battle of Fallen Timbers, after which thousands of white settlers begin pouring into Ohio and Indiana.

1803

Led by President Thomas Jefferson, the United States purchases the territory of Louisiana from France, roughly doubling the size of the country. This acquisition, followed up by the Lewis and Clark expedition (1803–1806), which explores the continent's western lands, initiates a new movement of white westward expansion into Indian-inhabited regions.

1812

War commences between the United States and Britain. Hoping to halt further U.S. expansion, Tecumseh and other Indian leaders ally themselves with the British.

1813

Tecumseh is killed in battle, effectively ending chances for a large pan-Indian crusade against the United States.

1813–1814

The Creek Wars, in which the United States defeats the Creek and forces most to move to Indian Country (encompassing much of what is now Missouri and Oklahoma), a region set aside for Indian relocation.

1821

Those Cherokee forced to relocate to Indian Country go to war with the Osage, who already occupy the region.

ca.1829

Goyathlay, the Apache war leader who will come to be known by the name given him by the Mexicans—Geronimo—is born.

1835

President Andrew Jackson publicly warns those Cherokee who have refused to relocate that they must do so or face dire consequences.

1835–1842

Some three thousand Seminole are shipped from Florida to Indian Country.

1838

U.S. troops forcibly remove the remaining Cherokee from their homes and lead them in a cruel forced march overland to Indian Country, an incident that becomes known as the "Trail of Tears."

1848

The Apache, Navajo, and many other Indians inhabiting the arid Southwest (what is now Arizona, New Mexico, and southern California) come under U.S. jurisdiction with the signing of the treaty ending the Mexican-American War.

1861–1865

The American Civil War.

1864

The United States defeats the Navajo and forces them to march to a relocation camp in eastern New Mexico. A Colorado regiment led by Colonel John M. Chivington massacres a group of Cheyenne and Arapaho at Sand Creek, in southeastern Colorado.

1876

The Sioux, aided by the Cheyenne and other Plains Indians, defeat General George Crook's forces at Rosebud Creek in southeastern Montana. A few days later, at the nearby Little Bighorn River, the allied Indians wipe out a force of over two hundred troops led by General George Armstrong Custer.

1877

Several hundred Nez Percé Indians, led by Chief Joseph, flee their assigned reservation in an attempt to reach Canada and freedom. They are captured only thirty miles from their goal. Meanwhile, some three hundred Cheyenne, led by Chief Dull Knife, attempt to return to their ancestral lands in Montana. They too are captured before attaining their goal.

1886

After many years of waging highly effective guerrilla warfare against frustrated U.S. troops, the last undefeated bands of Apache surrender.

1887

The U.S. Congress passes the General Allotment Act (or Dawes Act), which provides for the division of Indian reservations into tiny parcels to be homesteaded by Indian families.

1890

The Ghost Dance, a new religion that promises the destruction of the whites and salvation of the Indian race, spreads across the western plains. Sitting Bull, legendary Sioux chief, is shot and killed while being arrested on suspicion of inciting Indians to join the Ghost Dance. Soon afterward, U.S. troops massacre a large group of unarmed Indians at Wounded Knee Creek in South Dakota.

1934

Congress passes the Indian Reorganization Act, which ends allotment, reverses many of the Indian assimilation policies of the previous several decades, and allows Indians to form their own tribal governments on their reservations.

1973

Members of the American Indian Movement (AIM), a militant activist organization demanding better treatment for Indians, occupy the Pine Ridge Reservation, site of the Wounded Knee massacre, for seventy-one days. Two years later two FBI agents are killed in a shootout with Indian activists on the same reservation.

1978

Congress passes the American Indian Freedom of Religion Act, guaranteeing protection for Indian religious beliefs under the First Amendment.

For Further Research

Collections of Original Documents by or About Native Americans

Nancy B. Black and Bette S. Weidman, eds., *White on Red: Images of the American Indian.* Port Washington, NY: Kennikat Press, 1976.

Daniel Gookin, *Historical Collections of the Indians in New England.* N.p.: Towtaid, 1970.

Jerome A. Greene, ed., *Battles and Skirmishes of the Great Sioux War, 1876–1877: A Military View.* Norman: University of Oklahoma Press, 1993.

T.C. McLuhan, *Touch the Earth: A Self-Portrait of Indian Existence.* New York: Promontory Press, 1971.

Lee Miller, ed., *From the Heart: Voices of the American Indian.* New York: Random House, 1995.

Wayne Moquin, ed., *Great Documents in American Indian History.* New York: Da Capo Press, 1995.

Peter Nabokov, ed., *Native American Testimony.* New York: Harper and Row, 1978.

Annette Rosenstiel, *Red and White: Indian Views of the White Man, 1492–1982.* New York: Universe Books, 1983.

Edward H. Spicer, *A Short History of the Indians of the United States.* New York: D. Van Nostrand, 1969. Note: Contains an extensive collection of primary source documents.

William O. Taylor, *With Custer on the Little Bighorn.* New York: Viking, 1996. Note: This is the recently rediscovered memoir of a U.S. soldier who served under General Custer and had firsthand knowledge, much of it previously unknown, of the Little Bighorn campaign.

Frederick W. Turner, ed., *The Portable North American Indian Reader.* New York: Viking Press, 1974.

Wilcomb E. Washburn, ed., *The Indian and the White Man.* Garden City, NY: Doubleday, 1964.

Shirley H. Witt and Stan Steiner, eds., *The Way: An Anthology of American Indian Literature*. New York: Knopf, 1972.

General Histories and Studies of Native American Cultures

Betty Ballantine and Ian Ballantine, eds., *The Native Americans: An Illustrated History*. Atlanta: Turner, 1992.

Benjamin Capps, *The Indians*. New York: Time-Life Books, 1973.

Angie Debo, *A History of the Indians of the U.S.* Norman: University of Oklahoma Press, 1970.

Vine Deloria Jr., *God Is Red: A Native View of Religion*. Golden, CO: Fulcrum, 1994.

Peter Farb, *Man's Rise to Civilization as Shown by the Indians of North America from Primeval Times to the Coming of the Industrial State*. New York: E.P. Dutton, 1968.

Arrell M. Gibson, *The American Indian: Prehistory to the Present*. Lexington, MA: D.C. Heath, 1980.

Robert S. Grumet, ed., *Northeastern Indian Lives, 1632–1816*. Amherst: University of Massachusetts Press, 1996.

Royal B. Hassrick, *The Colorful Story of North American Indians*. London: Octopus Books, 1974.

Jamake Highwater, *Fodor's Indian America*. New York: David McKay, 1975.

Frederick E. Hoxie, ed., *Encyclopedia of North American Indians*. Boston: Houghton Mifflin, 1996.

George Hyde, *Indians of the High Plains*. Norman: University of Oklahoma Press, 1959.

Peter Iverson, *The Navajo Nation*. Albuquerque: University of New Mexico Press, 1981.

Alvin M. Josephy Jr., *The Indian Heritage of America*. New York: Knopf, 1968.

Beatrice Medicine and Patricia Albers, *The Hidden Half: Studies of Plains Indian Women*. Washington, DC: University Press of America, 1983.

Wendell H. Ostwalt and Sharlotte Neely, *This Land Was Theirs: A Study of North American Indians*. Mountain View, CA: Mayfield, 1996.

Carl Waldman, *Atlas of the North American Indian*. New York: Facts On File, 1985.

Evelyn Wolfson, *From Abenaki to Zuni: A Dictionary of Native American Tribes*. New York: Walker, 1988.

General Overviews of the Indian Wars

Norman Bancroft-Hunt, *Warriors: Warfare and the Native American Indian*. London: Salamander Books, 1995.

Cyrus T. Brady, *Indian Fights and Fighters*. Lincoln: University of Nebraska Press, 1971.

Ray Brandes, ed., *Troopers West: Military and Indian Affairs on the American Frontier*. San Diego: Frontier Heritage Press, 1970.

Dee Brown, *Bury My Heart at Wounded Knee: An Indian History of the American West*. New York: Holt, Rinehart, and Winston, 1970.

Wilbur R. Jacobs, *Dispossessing the American Indian: Indians and Whites on the Colonial Frontier*. New York: Scribner's, 1972.

John Keegan, *Fields of Battle: The Wars for North America*. New York: Knopf, 1996.

Stephen Longstreet, *War Cries on Horseback: The Story of the Indian Wars of the Great Plains*. New York: W.H. Allen, 1971.

S.L.A. Marshall, *Crimsoned Prairie: The Wars Between the United States and the Plains Indians During the Winning of the West*. New York: Scribner's, 1972.

J. Jay Myers, *Red Chiefs and White Challengers: Confrontations in American Indian History*. New York: Washington Square Press, 1971.

Don Nardo, *The Indian Wars*. San Diego: Lucent Books, 1991.

Michael P. Rogin, *Fathers and Children: Andrew Jackson and the Subjugation of the American Indian*. New York: Knopf, 1975.

Ian K. Steele, *Warpaths: Invasions of North America*. New York: Oxford University Press, 1994.

John Tebbel and Keith Jennison, *The American Indian Wars*. New York: Harper and Brothers, 1960.

Robert M. Utley and Wilcomb E. Washburn, *Indian Wars*. Boston: Houghton Mifflin, 1977.

Studies of Individual Wars, Battles, and Leaders

Gordon C. Baldwin, *The Warrior Apaches*. Tucson, AZ: Dale Stuart King, 1965.

David H. Cockran, *The Cherokee Frontier, Conflict and Survival*. Norman: University of Oklahoma Press, 1962.

Evan S. Connell, *Son of the Morning Star: Custer and the Little Bighorn*. San Francisco: North Point Press, 1984.

Carlton Culmsee, *Utah's Black Hawk War*. Logan: Utah State University Press, 1973.

John Ehle, *Trail of Tears: The Rise and Fall of the Cherokee Nation*. New York: Doubleday, 1988.

T.R. Fehrenbach, *Comanches: The Destruction of a People*. New York: Da Capo Press, 1994.

Lawrence M. Hauptman, *The Iroquois Struggle for Survival*. Syracuse, NY: Syracuse University Press, 1986.

Stanley Hoig, *The Sand Creek Massacre*. Norman: University of Oklahoma Press, 1961.

Jason Hook, *American Indian Warrior Chiefs: Tecumseh, Crazy Horse, Chief Joseph, Geronimo*. Dorset, UK: Firebird Books, 1990.

Helen A. Howard, *Saga of Chief Joseph*. Lincoln: University of Nebraska Press, 1965.

Elizabeth A. John, *Storms Brewed in Other Men's Worlds: The Confrontation of Indians, Spanish, and French in the Southwest, 1540–1795*. Norman: University of Oklahoma Press, 1996.

Charles H.L. Johnston, *Famous Indian Chiefs*. Freeport, NY: Books for Libraries Press, 1971.

James Mooney, *The Ghost Dance Religion and the Sioux Outbreak of 1890*. Lincoln: University of Nebraska Press, 1991.

Howard Pekham, *Pontiac and the Indian Uprising of 1763*. Princeton, NJ: Princeton University Press, 1947.

Mari Sandoz, *Crazy Horse, the Strange Man of the Oglalas*. New York: Knopf, 1945.

Edgar I. Stewart, *Custer's Luck*. Norman: University of Oklahoma Press, 1955.

John Sugden, *Tecumseh: A Life*. New York: Henry Holt, 1997.

Glen Tucker, *Tecumseh: Vision of Glory*. Indianapolis: Bobbs-Merrill, 1956.

Robert M. Utley, *The Last Days of the Sioux Nation*. New Haven, CT: Yale University Press, 1963.

Native American Problems and Struggles for Survival

Vine Deloria Jr., *Custer Died for Your Sins: An Indian Manifesto*. New York: Macmillan, 1969.

———, *Behind the Trail of Broken Treaties: An Indian Declaration of Independence*. New York: Delacorte Press, 1974.

Brian W. Dippie, *The Vanishing American: White Attitudes and U.S. Indian Policy*. Middletown, CT: Wesleyan University Press, 1982.

Gregory E. Dowd, *A Spirited Resistance: The North American Indian Struggle for Unity, 1745–1815*. Baltimore: Johns Hopkins University Press, 1992.

Grant Foreman, *Indian Removal*. Norman: University of Oklahoma Press, 1972.

Albert L. Hurtado and Peter Iverson, eds., *Major Problems in American Indian History*. Lexington, MA: D.C. Heath, 1994.

Paula M. Marks, *In a Barren Land: American Indian Dispossession and Survival*. New York: Morrow, 1998.

Roger L. Nichols and George R. Adams, eds., *The American Indian: Past and Present*. Lexington, MA: Xerox College, 1971.

Roger C. Owens et al., eds., *The North American Indians: A Sourcebook*. New York: Macmillan, 1967.

Raymond W. Steadman, *Shadows of the Indian: Stereotypes in American Culture*. Norman: University of Oklahoma Press, 1982.

Theodore Taylor, *The Bureau of Indian Affairs*. Boulder, CO: Westview Press, 1984.

Russell Thornton, *American Indian Holocaust and Survival: A Population History Since 1492*. Norman: University of Oklahoma Press, 1987.

William E. Unrau, *White Man's Wicked Water: The Alcohol Trade and Prohibition in Indian Country, 1802–1892*. Lawrence: University Press of Kansas, 1996.

Dale Van Every, *The Disinherited: The Lost Birthright of the American Indian*. New York: Morrow, 1976.

Wilcomb E. Washburn, *The Indian in America*. New York: Harper and Row, 1975.

Ronald Wright, *Stolen Continents: The Americas Through Indian Eyes Since 1492*. Boston: Houghton Mifflin, 1992.

Index